The Changing Civil Service

The Changing Civil Service

GEOFFREY K. FRY
University of Leeds

London
GEORGE ALLEN & UNWIN
Boston   Sydney

George Allen & Unwin (Publishers) Ltd,
40 Museum Street, London WC1A 1LU, UK

George Allen & Unwin (Publishers) Ltd,
Park Lane, Hemel Hempstead, Herts HP2 4TE, UK

Allen & Unwin, Inc.,
Fifty Cross Street, Winchester, Mass. 01890, USA

George Allen & Unwin Australia Pty Ltd,
8 Napier Street, North Sydney, NSW 2060, Australia

First published in 1985.

British Library Cataloguing in Publication Data

Fry, Geoffrey K.
   The changing Civil Service.
   1. Civil Service – Great Britain
   I. Title
   354.41006   JN425
   ISBN 0–04–350063–3
   ISBN 0–04–350064–1 Pbk

Library of Congress Cataloging in Publication Data

Fry, Geoffrey Kingdon.
   The changing civil service.
   Bibliography: p.
   Includes index.
   1. Civil Service – Great Britain. I. Title.
   JN425.F783   1984   354.41006   84–14579
   ISBN 0–04–350063–3 (alk. paper)
   ISBN 0–04–350064–1 (pbk.: alk. paper)

Set in 11 on 12 point Garamond by Phoenix Photosetting, Chatham
and printed in Great Britain
by Billing and Sons Ltd, London and Worcester

Contents

Preface

This is the second book which I have written about the British civil service. The first, *Statesmen in Disguise*, was published in 1969. It was a history of the administrative class of the home civil service from 1853 down to the Fulton Report. This second book is narrower in time-scale, since it primarily considers the period from Fulton onwards, but wider in the sense that it deals with a broader range of civil servants, including those of the diplomatic service and with issues such as civil service unionism and questions of pay.

The Changing Civil Service is *not* a text book. It is an interpretative essay of assessment. Not everybody will like the interpretation, especially as, while not hostile to 'reform', I decline to treat the Fulton Report as if it were equivalent to the Bible. It is treated as a very important State Paper. This book is not hostile to the civil service, to its unions, or to the notion that its members should be well paid. So, a simple-minded classification of this book as 'anti-Fulton' or 'anti-civil service' would be misguided. The interpretation presented is based on evidence.

That this book has had to be heavily selective in the areas covered is explained by its intentionally short length. This is the main reason why, for instance, I have usually grouped the references at the end of each paragraph, and why for the first time I have not included a long bibliography in one of my books. The statistics used are the fullest and the most up-to-date available at the time of writing. I am grateful to the Controller of Her Majesty's Stationery Office for general permission to quote from its published material; and to the editors of *Public Administration* for permission to use material previously published in that journal.

I take this opportunity to thank the many civil servants who have dealt so patiently with my inquiries, and to thank the highly professional civil service unions for their aid too. A further advantage has been the advice given by my talented friends and colleagues, James Macdonald and Owen Hartley. Of course, these scholars bear no responsibility for the contents of this book. That responsibility is solely mine. I take this opportunity also of thanking the staff of the Brotherton Library at Leeds, and especially Oliver Pickering, Maureen Cresswell and Janet Whitehouse, for their help.

Having dedicated earlier books to my parents, my wife and my children, I dedicate this book to my parents-in-law.

GEOFFREY K. FRY
September 1983

To Charles and Mary Hughes

1   The Changing Civil Service

The civil service is that body of men and women who work directly for ministers held to account in Parliament. It is essential, however, to realize that this body, large in number though it may seem, is but a small part of those who are paid out of public money. A broad definition of the civil service, for example, would include judges, the employees of public corporations and of the national health service, local government officers, teachers and nurses: but this hardly accounts for all the people engaged in public service. If we define the civil service to include all those people engaged in a public duty the total would far exceed, for instance, the 7·04 million who were formally employed in the public sector in 1982. For example, one would have to add to this total private sector employees computing PAYE. Members of the legal profession acting for clients in response to legal aid would have to be added in too. Even without such additions, it is evident that the scale of public employment has become massive. The total of 7·04 million given above represents a net increase of 1·2 million compared with 1961. The number of employees in the national health service more than doubled between 1961 and 1982 to reach a total of 1·3 million. The main net increase in that period, however, came in local authority employment where the numbers employed in education services and in health and personal social services appproximately doubled, in the former case to reach a total of 1·5 million. Local authorities employed a total of no less than 2·93 million in 1982 compared with 2·35 million in central government and 1·76 million in the public corporations. Public sector employment in Britain is of a similar scale to that in other Western European countries, accounting for about 30 per cent of total employment.[1]

The civil service only accounts for about 10 per cent of public employment, and the total number of civil servants has changed little since the days of the Priestley Report of 1955. Then the total was 719,000. By 1961 this was down to 643,000. At the beginning of 1982 there were 675,400 civil servants. However, these bare statistics hide a marked change in the composition of the civil service. While the service probably remains the largest single employer of skilled craftsmen in the country, the industrial staff (mainly ordnance factory, dockyard and workshop employees), which formed a majority of the civil service in 1939 and constituted about 46 per cent of its ranks in 1955, represented only about 23 per cent of the total number of civil servants in 1982. The number of industrial civil servants declined from 256,000 to 143,000 between 1961 and 1982 – a decline of 44 per cent. Over the same period the number of non-industrial civil servants rose from 387,000 to 533,000 – an increase of 38 per cent.[2]

This book is about the non-industrial civil service which, for the sake of brevity at the cost of strict accuracy, we shall call the civil service. This service includes in its ranks members of a wide range of professional and highly specialized occupations, including scientists drawn from nearly forty distinct disciplines. This is besides that majority of staff who are employed on administrative and clerical work, much of which is itself specialized. Such is the complexity of the structure of the service, the diversity of the work it does and the extent to which it is dispersed throughout the country, that an internal review suggested in 1975 that many, possibly most, civil servants do not know obvious facts about the service and the extent to which its character has changed in recent years. The more forgivable ignorance of outsiders perhaps explains why, even in the 1980s, the popular stereotype of the civil servant remains 'the pin-stripe suited, bowler-hatted, umbrella-carrying, Whitehall-working bureaucrat'. Given that about one-third of the non-industrial home civil service is under 30 and about 45 per cent of its ranks are female, and only a small minority of its staff work in Inner London, the middle-aged, male, Whitehall image is very misleading, as Sir Ian Bancroft, the then head of that service, pointed out in 1980.[3] Nevertheless, the durability of this image emphasizes the need to establish certain basic facts about the service at the outset.

While the 532,805 non-industrial civil servants employed in 1982 were dispersed among sixty government departments, almost all of those departments employed small numbers of them. The number of staff is not always a reliable indicator of a department's relative importance – the Treasury only employed 2,579 such civil servants in 1982. None the less, the concentration of non-industrial civil servants in a handful of government departments is one remarkable fact to emerge from the official statistics. About 82 per cent of such civil servants in 1982 were employed in seven departments or closely related groups of departments – the Ministry of Defence (110,300 or 21 per cent); the Department of Health and Social Security (DHSS) (96,600 or 18 per cent); the Board of Inland Revenue (73,000 or 14 per cent); the Department of Employment (DE) group (56,800 or 11 per cent); the

Department of the Environment (DoE) including the Property Services Agency and Transport (36,900 or 7 per cent); the Home Office (31,100 or 6 per cent); and the Board of Customs and Excise (26,400 or 5 per cent). When industrial civil servants are included, the Ministry of Defence still actually employed 32 per cent of all civil servants in 1982. The number of non-industrial civil servants employed there, however, had fallen by 27,000 compared with the total working in defence departments in 1961. Changes in the machinery of government make such comparisons difficult, but between 1961 and 1982 all the other departments listed above showed an increase in the number of non-industrial civil servants that they employed. The DHSS area grew by 42,000, the DE group by 37,000, the Home Office by 19,000, the DoE area by 16,000, the Inland Revenue by 15,000, and the Customs and Excise by 11,000. The figures are approximate, but the changing pattern in the deployment of non-industrial civil servants between departments is much what one would expect. The main increases in staff are in the social security area (90 per cent of the DHSS staff are allocated to such work); the employment or, increasingly since 1966, the unemployment field; law and order and immigration control; the supervision of the growth area of local government; and the administration of taxation. The main reason why, for example, the non-industrial staff of the Customs and Excise increased by 41 per cent between 1961 and 1982 was that the number of registered traders under Value Added Tax (VAT) was about thirteen times as great as under purchase tax.[4]

So, looking particularly at the roles of the leading employing departments, the non-industrial civil service is bound to be a widely dispersed body and not one mainly located in and around Whitehall. Far from being concentrated there, such civil servants are employed all over Britain, working in over 7,000 buildings and sites. Some of these accommodate only half a dozen staff or fewer. At the other extreme the central office of the DHSS employs 10,000 staff in Longbenton, near Newcastle upon Tyne, on a 60-acre site that may well be the largest single office complex outside the USA, and the largest computer installation in Europe. Some 74 per cent of non-industrial civil servants work outside Greater London, 25 per cent work in Greater London (about 17 per cent in Inner London) and 1 per cent overseas. About 29 per cent work in headquarters offices, 7 per cent in regional offices, and 44 per cent in local offices. Four out of every nine such civil servants work in local offices which have some direct contact with the public. Many civil servants are entirely engaged in local casework – computing income tax, placing people in employment, or administering social security benefits.[5]

The character of the civil service has been considerably changed by the

The character of the civil service has been considerably changed by the expansion of local and regional office systems consequent upon the extension of government functions in the economic and social policy spheres, compounded by past government policies of office dispersal away from London. As an internal review observed in 1975: 'Over the years, the Civil Service has become increasingly a regional and local service and many, particularly in the lower grades, never move away from the area in which they were recruited; they retain their regional roots, and do not naturally associate themselves with the business of government in London.' In many parts of the service, 'the majority do not have white collar attitudes, and do not aspire to them'. The tone of the service has changed:

> Older civil servants joined when recruitment was highly competitive; before the War some schools would inscribe on the honours board the name of a boy who was accepted into the Civil Service as an Executive Officer; he had joined a small elite by open competition – in one year, for example, fourteen eligible candidates were turned away for each one who was accepted. But other jobs have become attractive and more widely available to those who meet the Service's recruitment standards, and today the very much larger numbers of Executive Officer entrants do not regard the Civil Service or themselves as very special.[6]

It is only a short step from regarding a civil service job as being like any other job to civil servants behaving like other employees, not least when it came to the conduct of industrial relations; a tendency accentuated by the dispersal of the service into areas of traditional union militancy.

The character of the civil service was continuing to change even as the Fulton Committee reviewed the main part of it between 1966 and 1968, and Fulton certainly did not anticipate the discarding of the old courtesies of Whitleyism that occurred in the 1970s. Fulton said that Whitleyism in the service had made 'an invaluable contribution to good staff relations. The high morale of the staff and the fact that industrial disputes are rare in the Civil Service, owe a great deal to the universal acceptance of the principle of joint consultation. . . . It is very much in the public interest that this atmosphere of agreement and of co-operation should be preserved.' In fact, the civil service staff associations were in the process of translating themselves into trade unions much like any other unions perhaps better so to represent those civil servants who saw themselves as being much like other employees. The moving spirit in this change was W. L. Kendall, then general secretary of the Civil and Public Services Association, the largest association, who marked the fiftieth anniversary of Whitleyism in 1969 by denouncing the system, and who led his union and then helped to lead the other unions in the 1973 and 1979 civil service strikes which undermined it. The election of a Conservative government in 1979, which believed civil service pay and conditions to be too generous, and which was determined to cut the size of the service by 100,000 down to 630,000 by April 1984, ensured further conflict. In 1980 Mr Kendall said: 'I am in the middle of a war with the Government.'[7] That unions representing civil servants could wage 'war' against an elected government raises important constitutional issues. So, in Chapter 6 of this book we shall examine the changing character of civil service unionism.

The immediate *casus belli* in 1981 between the unions and the Thatcher government was the latter's decision to dispense with the existing civil service pay arrangements. While Fulton's proposed structural changes in the service had implications for pay, the committee was clear about its endorsement of the principle of basing civil service salaries primarily on 'fair comparison' with pay in outside employment, as laid down by the Priestley Royal Commission of 1953–5. In Fulton's opinion, 'this principle remains valid and will continue to be necessary to the efficiency as well as to the contentment of the Service'. The Priestley system, in fact, rarely worked as smoothly as Fulton seemed to think and, in 1969 Mr Kendall chose to describe its operations as resulting in a 'brutal form of robbery' of his members.[8] Public criticism of the principle that civil servants should have comparable pay with outsiders, while remaining largely immune from redundancy, naturally grew with rising unemployment, much as resentment at civil servants having index-linked pensions increased with inflation. The 'counter-revolution' in economic thinking which occurred in the 1970s restored an older view of public money to predominance than had been fashionable at the time of Priestley. The Balanced Budget was back in favour, if not yet in practice, and an obvious way of trying to reduce public expenditure was to cut the number of civil servants and their cost. The Thatcher government's reaction was to get rid of the Priestley system and, eventually, to set up the Megaw Committee to recommend new arrangements. In Chapter 5 I shall examine the changing civil service pay system.

Attitudes towards public money have tended to determine the divisions always to be seen on the question of the location of the central management of the main part of the civil service. Almost all the unions and almost all the academics and many civil servants have traditionally wanted central management to be taken away from the Treasury, with its reputation for 'prudent housekeeping' supposedly always inclining it to resist worthwhile reforms and developments and, more basically, 'better' pay deals for civil servants. Although the 1962-style Treasury seemed positive enough, Fulton insisted that moving central management functions to a new Civil Service Department (CSD) was a pre-condition for the proper implementation of its reform programme. The Labour government duly obliged later in 1968. Given that the Treasury still had to find the money for the civil service, the duplication involved in establishing the CSD, while it tended to be ignored in the indulgent climate towards public expenditure even of the late 1960s, was less readily tolerated as the 1970s progressed. Far from the CSD pressing ahead with the Fulton reforms, its permanent secretary, Sir William Armstrong, was believed by one of Fulton's stars, Lord Crowther-Hunt, to have blocked the proposals for the whole service to have a unified grading structure.[9] Industrial relations worsened rather than improved. The CSD's efforts to promote greater efficiency in government departments showed few results. This served to emphasize how independent the other departments were and, given their overall scale, raised questions about how effectively central management could be exercised in the future, and even about the possible break-up of the civil service. The CSD, bereft of a serious role to play, was abolished by the Thatcher government in 1981. In Chapter 4 I shall examine the central management of the civil service question.

Treating the Fulton Report as the test of change is one reason why even among the interested public the prevailing impression is that 'the structure, recruitment and management, including training, of the Home Civil Service' – to quote Fulton's terms of reference[10] – are little changed now compared with 1968. This interpretation tends to ignore the fact that important changes in the service were well under way before Fulton, and that they have not been confined to within its guidelines since. In the area of direct-entry recruitment, the Civil Service Commission still strives to attract the best university products and all eyes turn to the competitions concerned, often ignoring the fact that, otherwise, such recruitment is dominated by departments, now without even formal approval from the commission. An important unifying thread in the civil service has been largely broken and one notes, too, that departments dominate the provision of post-entry training. The Civil Service College, as conceived by Fulton, never represented a radical change anyway and experience has borne this out. Nevertheless, compared with before 1968, the scale of post-entry training available to civil servants is substantially greater. As for structure, the mergers of the early 1970s on the generalist side of the service and in the major specialist groups followed Fulton's recommendations and almost everybody else's predictions. At that time, the creation of the unified grading structure that Fulton proposed – the introduction of which would have been a radical change – was only taken down as far as under secretary level. If Sir William Armstrong was obstructive only delay was bought, because in 1983 the Thatcher government, determined to rationalize the service, announced proposals to take unified grading further. In Chapter 3 I shall examine the changes which have taken place, particularly since 1968, in the structure of the civil service and in its recruitment and training arrangements, and, not being confined to the home civil service, as Fulton was, that examination will include the diplomatic service too.

The most important restriction on Fulton was its preclusion from examining the place of the civil service in the machinery of government. From the outset, the committee was hamstrung by being required to review the home civil service while not being allowed to fully examine the doctrine of ministerial responsibility which governs that service's work. Interesting proposals were made by Fulton, such as those relating to policy planning units, and a good deal was said *sotto voce*: but the committee could not properly consider the modern working of the minister–civil servant relationship. This would have been a crippling restriction at any time, but it was all the more a handicap in the Fulton era because by then it had come to be conventional wisdom that the influence of the civil service had increased, was increasing and ought to be diminished. Fulton criticized the administrative tone of the civil service – 'the cult of the amateur', and so on – but it could not fully relate this either to the effect of parliamentary requirements on the work of government departments, or to the style of British party politics which remains adamantly amateurish in the sphere of policy preparation. If the civil service was not under sufficient political control then ministers might well be to blame, and if parties declined to prepare adequately for office that was not the service's fault. Many saw things differently and, since Fulton, from both sides of the main party divide there have come calls for a politicized higher civil service, reflecting the belief that the service does not act as the politically neutral instrument in practice that constitutional theory implies. We now turn to an examination of the place of the higher civil service in the machinery of government.

References

1   M. Semple, 'Employment in the public and private sectors 1961–1978', *Economic Trends*, no. 313 (November 1979), pp. 90–108; E. Lomas, 'Employment in the public and private sectors 1974–1980', *Economic Trends*, no. 325 (November 1980), pp. 101–9; E. Lomas, 'A comparison of public services employment in the United Kingdom with five other European countries', *Economic Trends*, no. 326 (December 1980), pp. 94–100; H. Morrison, 'Employment in the public and private sectors 1976–1982', *Economic Trends*, no. 352 (February 1983), pp. 82–9.

2   *Civil Service Statistics 1971*, p. 14; *Civil Service Statistics 1982*, p. 9; M. J. Harvey, 'The industrial civil service', *Management in Government*, vol. 38 (1983), pp. 20–7.

3   *Civil Servants and Change. Joint Statement by the National Whitley Council and Final Report by the Wider Issues Review Team* (1975), pp. 4–5; Sir I. Bancroft, 'The civil service in the 1980s', *Public Administration*, vol. 59 (1981), pp. 139–40.

4   *Civil Service Statistics 1982*, pp. 9, 17; *Whitley Bulletin*, March 1962, pp. 46, 48; *Eleventh Report from the Expenditure Committee. The Civil Service* (English Report), HC 535–II (1976–7), p. 336; D. Johnstone, *A Tax Shall Be Charged*, Civil Service Studies no. 1 (1975), p. 7.

5   CSD, *The Civil Service: Introductory Factual Memorandum Submitted to the House of Commons Treasury and Civil Service Committee* (1980), p. 4; *Civil Servants and Change*, p. 4; W. G. Wilson, 'The management of Newcastle Central Office', *Management Services in Government*, vol. 36 (1981), p. 38.

6   *Civil Servants and Change*, p. 5.

7   *Report of the Committee on the Civil Service* (Fulton Report), Cmnd 3638 (1968), para. 270; *Red Tape*, December 1969, pp. 69–70; *The Times*, 12 August 1980.

8   Fulton Report, para. 226; *Red Tape*, December 1969, p. 70.

9   P. Kellner and Lord Crowther-Hunt, *The Civil Servants. An Inquiry into Britain's Ruling Class* (London, 1980), pp. 59–77.

10 Fulton Report, p. 2.

2 The Higher Civil Service in the Machinery of Government

'The constitutional responsibility of Ministers to Parliament and the public covers every action of the department, whether done with their specific authority or by delegation, expressed or implied', Sir Edward Bridges, the then permanent secretary to the Treasury and head of the home civil service, wrote in 1950. A similar note of certainty about the minister–civil servant relationship to that which Bridges struck, and which he matched then and later in the 1950s in publicly extolling the virtues of the 'generalist' as the ideal higher civil servant, is not to be easily detected now. The higher civil service has taken at least its share of the blame for the economic difficulties which Britain has experienced since the 1950s. That service's formal subordination to political control has proved to be little protection, because the belief that the convention of ministerial responsibility is a 'myth' has come to be a commonplace in discussion of British government. A consequence of this is that, compared with Bridges' day, the interested public displays considerable disrespect for the 'generalist' administrator whose expertise is in running the traditional apparatus connected with the doctrine of ministerial responsibility. The Fulton Report reflected this disrespect. Its opening chapter vigorously attacked the 'generalist', placing it first in a long list of failings which it believed that the service had demonstrated in its organization and work. This list was similar to that which Fabian reformers such as Harold Laski and W. A. Robson had advanced in the past. The confidence with which criticism had been rebuffed, more often ignored, then was less and less evident as, consequent upon still further relative national economic decline, the political climate became even more unfavourable to the civil service as the 1970s progressed. Looking back from the Treasury over his own career, and with Bridges in mind, Sir Douglas Wass recorded in 1983 that the mood of the Service today . . . lacks the assurance which our predecessors took as given'. He recognized that 'people are worried about a host of questions: the size and efficiency of the Service; its standards of performance; its accountability for its acts of commission and omission; the state of its industrial relations; the privileges it is held to enjoy; and the objectives it sets itself.' A politicized higher civil service is now on the reformers' agenda on both sides of the main political divide.[1] So, the former certainties have gone, while, at the same time, the practical requirements of the British form of parliamentary democracy – unhelpfully placed outside Fulton's remit – have still to be met by the civil service. These requirements demand that higher civil servants possess certain skills, but not necessarily that they adhere to 'the cult of the generalist'. Thus, how that 'cult' became established is an essential element in an examination of the part that the higher civil service plays in the machinery of government.

1   The Warren Fisher Inheritance: 'The Cult of the Generalist'

'The Home Civil Service today is still fundamentally the product of the nineteenth century philosophy of the Northcote–Trevelyan Report. The tasks it faces are those of the second half of the twentieth century. This is what we have found; it is what we seek to remedy.' Thus the Fulton Committee opened its report in 1968 in the belief that

> the Service is still essentially based on the philosophy of the amateur (or 'generalist' or 'all rounder'). This is most evident in the Administrative Class which holds the dominant position in the Service. The ideal administrator is still too often seen as the gifted layman who, moving frequently from job to job within the Service, can take a practical view of any problem, irrespective of its subject matter, in the light of his knowledge and experience of the government machine . . . The cult is obsolete at all levels and in all parts of the Service.

Sixty years before, Professor A. L. Lowell from Harvard had portrayed the role of the civil service in British central government rather differently. He believed that 'any work . . . carried on at the present day without the assistance of experts is certain to be more or less inefficient. But, on the other hand, experts acting alone tend to take disproportionate views . . . In order, therefore, to produce really good results, and avoid the dangers of inefficiency on the one hand, and of bureaucracy on the other, it is necessary to have in any administration a proper combination of experts and men of the world.' Lowell saw ministers as providing 'the lay element in the concern'; the civil servants played the role of 'confidential expert'.[2] Fulton was not prepared to concede the title of 'expert' to the civil service administrators of 1968; and as the former's views had supporting evidence and the latter's were not lacking in perception, it is reasonable to conclude that the 'cult' came to the fore sometime in the intervening sixty years. Its main architect was to be found in the Treasury, but it was neither Sir Charles Trevelyan in the 1850s nor, despite much publicity, Sir Edward Bridges in the 1950s. The High Priest of 'the cult of the generalist' was the now largely forgotten figure of Sir Warren Fisher, the head of the civil service in the 1920s and 1930s.

'Until relatively recent years the expression "Civil Service" did not correspond either to the spirit or to the facts of the organization so described', Fisher told the Tomlin Commission in 1930.

> There was a series of departments with conditions of service which in quite important respects differed materially; departments did not really think of themselves as merely units of a complete and correlated whole; and in the recognition by each department of the existence of others there was, from time to time, an attitude of superiority, of condescension, of resentment, or even of suspicion. Such departmentalism is, of course, the antithesis of a 'Service'.

However, Fisher believed, 'the evolution of a Service conception in contrast to the merely departmental one has of late years progressed some distance'. Here was an interpretation of civil service history from a man well aware that he was helping to shape it: but it does seem clear that, without suggesting that they were ever fully realized, the Trevelyan–Northcote ambitions for a unified civil service were frustrated before about 1920. A 'cult of the generalist' may well have been latent before that, given that, as Trevelyan–Northcote wished, the open competitions from 1870 onwards were designed to attract 'young men of general ability, which is a matter of more moment than their being possessed of any special acquirements'. However, as the service retained the 'fragmentary character' which Trevelyan–Northcote had deplored, the entrants to the First Division – as the 'intellectual' class came to be called – were assigned to a particular department, sometimes even into a specific branch of it, and normally stayed there for the remainder of their working lives. This was a career pattern that, over time, tended to encourage the 'expertise' that Lowell had detected. It was an 'expertise' born of long experience and one more compatible with ministerial responsibility than a service with men of independent reputation like Sir Edwin Chadwick or Sir John Simon could ever be.[3]

What translated the old 'fragmented' First Division into the 'generalist' administrative class was the National Health Insurance 'adventure' of 1911–12 which broke down some departmental barriers, the First World War which broke down some more, and the activities of Sir Warren Fisher at the head of the Treasury and of the service for almost all of the interwar period. For Fisher, involvement in the Health Insurance episode was the crucial experience. Talent was drawn from all over the First Division to make the scheme work on time. Fisher himself was brought in from the Board of Inland Revenue and into close working contact with exotics like Sir Robert Morant, whose style he may later have tried to emulate, and Lloyd George, who, as Prime Minister, placed Fisher, barely 40 years old, at the top of the service in October 1919. Fisher became permanent secretary to the Treasury and head of the civil service. In this latter role he received unprecedented formal powers to advise the Prime Minister on honours and on appointments in all departments to the posts of permanent secretary, deputy secretary, principal financial officer and principal establishment officer. Fisher's writ included the Foreign Office and the diplomatic service. Fisher's interventions in this area and that of defence were controversial. They culminated in Fisher unsuccessfully recommending himself to Neville Chamberlain as the best successor available to Sir Robert Vansittart as permanent under secretary at the Foreign Office. Fisher's flamboyant behaviour, which eventually surfaced in public, seems to have detracted attention from his central role in advancing 'the cult of the generalist'. The eye tends to be drawn to Sir Edward Bridges. However, Bridges was only just entering the service in 1919 when Fisher successfully pressed his view that the grading and salary structure of what was to become the administrative class should be standardized and that the class should be treated as a *corps d'élite* capable of being employed anywhere in the service. Fisher, sensitive to charges that the civil service had been a haven in times of slaughter, was fond of treating the service as being like the armed forces – comparing the leading civil servants with the General Staff. Some departments were affected only to a limited extent by Fisher's interventions, possibly reflecting his interests – the Board of Education being an important example – but elsewhere Fisher played what he literally called 'musical chairs' in filling the highest posts in the civil service. For he was not restrained by any belief that lack of expertise in the work of departments was a handicap to experienced administrators, believing that such men could run any department.[4]

The Warren Fisher inheritance left the civil service with a distinctive style of administration. This was often portrayed by others — like Fulton later — as amateurism: but Fisher's contemporary, H. E. Dale, speaking from experience, was clear that the high official was 'an expert in a difficult art, the detailed working of the central government in British parliamentary democracy'. What the higher civil servant specialized in, a later practitioner, C. H. Sisson wrote, was 'the awareness of ministerial responsibility'.[5] This necessary expertise, though, was compatible with departmentalism. Having the entire higher civil service as a career prospect instead of being confined within departmental walls (unless they were those of the Treasury) was an obvious enticement to the ambitious civil servant. Fisher seemed to relish the powers of patronage involved too. Nevertheless, the move away from departmentalism has not been accompanied by any diminution in the complexity of the subject matters dealt with by departments, and hence for the need for specialized knowledge of these matters, rather the opposite. The prime characteristic of the Warren Fisher dispensation, which was eventually handed on to Sir Edward Bridges, who gloried in it, was that 'the lay element' which Lowell had seen ministers providing was dominant on the civil service side, too, as Fulton found.

2   The Doctrine of Ministerial Responsibility and the Higher Civil Service

The Principle of Ministerial Responsibility

'The Minister in charge of the department is answerable to Parliament for the workings of the department. The action of the department is action for which the department is collectively responsible and for which the Minister in charge is alone answerable to Parliament', Sir Elwyn Jones told a House of Commons Select Committee in 1968, in the wake of the Foreign Office having been criticized by the Ombudsman for maladministration in the Sachsenhausen case. He added that 'it is only in exceptional cases that blame should be attached to the individual civil servant and it follows from the principle that the Minister alone has responsibility for the actions of the department that the individual civil servant who has contributed to the collective decision of the department should remain anonymous'. In the year of Fulton, the then Attorney-General was advancing what remains the latest definition of the doctrine of ministerial responsibility to gain entry into the constitutional law books.[6] It was a markedly more defensive definition than that which we saw that Sir Edward Bridges had given nearly twenty years before. While the collective responsibility of the Cabinet was, and is, an established convention of the constitution, the notion of the collective responsibility of civil servants in a department was novel. Perhaps, as the consequences of the Crichel Down affair led on to the establishment of the Ombudsman and thence to the Sachsenhausen case, it was the civil servants who feared that, if they did not hang together, they would hang separately. If so, such caution was justified for, in the period since, there has been no close season in the hunting of the civil service, the hunters being spurred on by the belief that ministerial responsibility is a constitutional 'fiction'.

The doctrine of ministerial responsibility is *not* a myth. It is the principle around which the core of British central government and, hence, the work of the civil service, is organized. The Fulton Committee was thus hamstrung when the Labour government of 1966 prevented it from properly examining the current working of the convention of ministerial responsibility. The marking out of this territory as forbidden meant that Fulton was formally sentenced to hop around its subject. When the committee strayed on to this territory, its most interesting recommendations followed. For, as Edmund Dell, a former Labour minister, said in 1980, 'the most important form of responsibility within a Government is the responsibility of a Minister for the conduct of his own department . . . That . . . should be the foundation of government.' In principle, it is. Ministerial resignations over matters of policy and administration have always been rare:[7] but ministers still remain responsible in the sense that they are liable to report upon the activities of the government department of which they are a political head to the Crown, to the Prime Minister and Cabinet, and to Parliament. Civil servants remain non-political in the sense that they normally receive their appointments independently of ministers, that they are not allowed an overt political allegiance and that they are not required to perform politically on the floor of either House of Parliament. Civil servants are required to appear before parliamentary committees, but they are still neither publicly responsible for the advice that they have given to ministers, nor for the efficiency with which they carry out their work.

The Higher Civil Service, its Critics and the Myth of 'the Common Ground'
To the question of 'what is wanted and expected from the Higher Civil Service?' H. E. Dale wrote in 1941, there was 'only one answer possible, both in constitutional theory and in fact' — namely, that which was wanted and expected 'by Ministers'. Plainly, Dale was

confident that ministers would 'want and expect' much the same kind of higher civil service and leading administrator within its ranks as the Warren Fisher inheritance had bequeathed them. For over twenty years now, however, the Dale–Sisson administrator has been out of fashion. The Plowden Report on the Control of Public Expenditure said in 1961 that a greater emphasis on management was needed in the higher reaches of the service, and Fulton said much the same. Fulton and others have cast envious eyes at French technocracy. Recent Labour and Conservative governments have proved less willing than their predecessors to rely solely on civil service advisers, bringing political appointees within departments, sometimes at senior levels. One of their number, Sir John Hoskyns, who, for three years, had been senior policy adviser to Mrs Thatcher, declared in 1982 that few of the leading officials in the higher civil service over 50 were much good, not least because they were imbued with a defeatist outlook. So, to make the Whitehall culture more positive, these civil servants needed to be pensioned off, to be replaced by outsiders, mainly from business, who would give ministers capable, highly motivated political support.[8] While unfavourable comparisons with the supposed greater efficiency of private enterprise are familiar ingredients of Conservative criticisms of the civil service, the Hoskyns solution of a mass clear-out of its highest ranks had more novelty. It also meant that the higher civil service was being assailed from both right and left at the same time. For, on the opposite side of the political fence from Hoskyns, what we may call the Harold Laski inheritance was flourishing. Not just the usual complaints about Oxbridge-dominated administrative recruitment, deficient training and the 'closed' nature of the service (about which, of course, Hoskyns was proposing something should be done). Very much alive, too, was the belief that, not least because of its social tone, the higher civil service was obstructive to Labour governments, indeed a prime cause of their 'failures'. This belief was evident in the Minority Report of the English Committee on the civil service of 1976–7 in which the influence of Tony Benn's ally, Brian Sedgemore, could be detected, and in the subsequent writings of Sedgemore and Benn.

The Benn thesis, first advanced in developed form in 1980, is that in recent years, and particularly since membership of the EEC – the Brussels bureaucracy being 'a mandarin's paradise' – the power of the higher civil service has grown to such an extent that it threatens the future of the British system of parliamentary government. Benn's argument was that the Civil Service has

> a political position of its own to defend against all-comers, including incoming Governments armed with their philosophy and programme.

Civil Service policy . . . is an amalgam of views that have been developed over a long period. It draws some of its force from a deep commitment to the benefits of continuity and a fear that adversary politics may lead to sharp reversals by incoming Governments of policies devised by their predecessors, which the Civil Service played a greater part in developing. To that extent, the Permanent Secretaries could be expected to prefer consensus politics and to hope that such a consensus would remain the basis for all policy and administration. As the term implies, consensus politics draws its inspiration from many sources in all political parties. The post-war consensus, which ended during the 1970s, was based upon the foundation laid by the Liberal Government of 1906 . . . Consensus politics was institutionalized during the wartime Coalition, in which Winston Churchill and Clement Attlee worked together. Despite the heated political debates of the 1950s and 1960s this broad consensus remained, in that the disagreements between the parties were contained within the framework of agreed objectives such as full employment and a Welfare State. The differences were largely then confined to the question of which party was to be privileged to administer these policies. The Civil Service laboured long and hard in support of this approach and helped to construct a top level corporate structure of committees and quangos, which brought together all those who could be persuaded to share their desire for the minimum of public controversy that is compatible with the two-and-a-half party system. Thus, when the senior civil servants see a new Government come into power with a policy that goes outside that consensus, there is anxiety at the possible effect upon their own policy. Plans are laid, that seek to contain this new surge of political power and divert ministerial energies into safer channels that do not disturb the even flow of established Whitehall policy.

Benn has seen 'this process of Civil Service containment successfully practised against both Conservative and Labour Governments over the last thirty years'. It was the main reason why 'Governments of both parties appear to end up with policies very similar to each other; and which are in every case a great deal more acceptable to Whitehall than were the manifestos upon which they were originally elected'. Both Labour and Conservative members of the English Committee observed that

all civil servants naturally say that they exist solely to serve the Government and that they take their policy instructions automatically from Ministers . . . However, many who have been, or who are, Ministers believe that Ministers do not always get the service which it is claimed that they get. They say that they find on their coming into office that some departments have firmly held policy views and that it is very difficult to change these views. When they are changed, the department will often try and reinstate its own policies through the passage of time and the erosion of Ministers' political will. Many departments are large and it is not difficult to push forward policies without a Minister's knowledge, particularly if there is any lack of clarity in defining demarcation lines between different Ministers' responsibilities, as has been known to happen. Further it is often said to be extremely difficult to launch a new policy initiative which is not to the liking of a department. Delay and obstruction are said to be among the tactics used, together with briefing Ministers in other departments to oppose the initiative in Cabinet or Cabinet Committee. The workload on Ministers is immense and procrastination or repetition of the difficulties of a policy would be tactics that Ministers would find difficulty in overcoming.

The English Minority said much the same with greater force, as did Mr Benn himself, stressing the officials' tactic of denying vital information to the minister. Benn believed that major constitutional reforms were urgently required, designed to 'restore the authority of the House of Commons, secure effective ministerial control over the Civil Service and move towards a more constitutional type of premiership'. A Freedom of Information Act was at the top of Benn's list.[9]

While Benn's views merit consideration because they are based on an interpretation of several years of experience as Cabinet minister, like most such criticisms they bear the Laski hallmark, as well as perhaps reflecting the old belief that, whatever party wins the elections, 'the Liberals are always in power'. G. W. E. Russell, a former Liberal Cabinet minister, wrote in 1903 that 'the Civil Service has no politics, but many of its members are staunch Liberals'. H. E. Dale's estimate from the inside in the interwar period was that 'in their political principles, not always expressed by their votes, about one-fourth of the Higher Civil Service are Conservative, one half or slightly more are Liberal, and the remainder Labour of one shade or another'. Dale said that 'the general temper of mind and character is Left Centre', but he was at pains to emphasize that higher civil servants loyally served their ministers whatever their political allegiance. Laski was not prepared to accept this pledge of political neutrality, believing that at that time it had not really been tested. 'Liberal Government could succeed Conservative Government before 1924 with the assurance to business men that the basic economic structure of our society would be undisturbed', Laski wrote in 1938. The advent of a Labour Party committed to socialism was something different from the Conservative and Liberal parties. It did call the private enterprise system into question. Laski cast doubt on the extent to which the higher civil service would co-operate with the implementation of a socialist manifesto of the kind which he believed the Short Programme of 1937 to be. Similarly, Laski doubted if the Foreign Office would really implement a socialist foreign policy. The reasons for this were supposed to lie in the civil servants' privileged social and educational backgrounds, Oxbridge and so on. Similar views appear in socialist tracts to this day and were present, for instance, in an interesting book about the Labour governments of 1964–70 written by the personal and political secretary to the Prime Minister, Marcia Williams. She believed that 'a glance at the Service, and particularly recruitment at higher levels, makes it quite impossible to accept the neutrality arguments'. The Wilson governments had been beaten by 'The System' which was 'in the hands of the upper grades of the Service'. Mrs Williams felt that the civil service was 'undemocratic, particularly at the top; exclusive; and with a strange personality of its own, half reminiscent of the Army, half of a masonic society. Certainly many of the members of the Administrative Class seem unrelated to the outside world.' Oxbridge, middle-class, privately educated, rarely drawn from 'north of Luton', Mrs Williams believed the administrative class to be natural allies of the Conservative Party. A survey associated with the Fulton inquiry, in fact, found that the 1956 entry into the administrative class contained a preponderance of Labour voters, although, of course, that entry may have been untypical for the sample was a small one and it was made in 1966, one of Labour's best years. Later experience in government and further reflection led Mrs Williams to think that the political outlook of the higher civil service had changed and that it had become best represented by the Liberal–Social Democratic Party Alliance which fought the 1983 election.[10]

The still influential 'Laski view' appears to rest on a simple correlation between higher civil servants having socially privileged backgrounds and Oxbridge educations which are said to lead them inevitably to have a class interest inimical to that of the Labour Party. It does seem strange how social critics and Labour leaders avoid behaving similarly, given that their origins are often much the same unlike the impeccable working-class credentials of, say, Ramsay

MacDonald. When one considers the familiar target of the diplomatic service, a further irony is that Guy Burgess and Donald Maclean, the diplomats who spied for and later defected to the Soviet Union in 1951, were the very class archetypes at whom Laski directed his fire. Yet, both certainly did their utmost for what they defined as socialism, as did 'Kim' Philby. Laski seemed to find sinister the well-known rapport that existed between the proletarian Ernest Bevin and the Foreign Office. The 'Laski view' tends to be expressed in a sufficiently generalized form to be incapable of substantiation – or refutation. Possibly there is something to be said for the opposing view that the Foreign Office and the diplomatic service are predominantly anti-Tory, a conclusion reached at least by Sir Geoffrey Jackson, a career diplomat, in memoirs published in 1981. Sir Geoffrey wrote that

> there are enough ex-Foreign Office Conservative MPs, or MEPs, to testify that a diplomat with an active Conservative motivation can always leave diplomacy in the hope of becoming a Douglas Hurd or a Ray Whitney, to name but two. Conversely Lord George-Brown's memoirs do not disguise the highly personal nature of some of his diplomatic appointments; one in particular he traces back to a future Ambassador's wife having publicly taken a partisan stance in his defence and presence. Similarly the widow of another Ambassador has asserted to the media that her husband, like herself, had approached each new post as a committed socialist.

With evident distaste, Sir Geoffrey seemed to think that there was some substance to the belief that, in recent times at least, 'under a Labour Government the ambitious FO man takes care to make known his allegiance to them. He does so in the full knowledge that when the Conservatives are back in power, he will not be penalized or his promotion affected.' Sir Geoffrey recorded that 'it was common knowledge that two-thirds of the Foreign Office and Service voted Labour nowadays . . . The wrong is only if they make it known, which more than one colleague has confirmed is commonplace.' Sir Geoffrey Jackson's remarks – made before the SDP split – are those of an experienced 'insider' about his fellow diplomats, and while they are impressionistic they are not more so than the 'Laski view'. If such observations do not constitute a rebuttal of left-wing suspicions they do at least require some explanation from such critics.[11]

Both Conservative and Labour governments were required to follow 'Civil Service policy', according to Mr Benn: hence, the U-turns made by the Wilson government in 1966, the Heath government in 1972 and the Wilson government again in 1975. The English Committee's Minority believed in 1977 that 'it is a matter of record and observation that civil servants obstructed the radical Selsdon Man policies' of the Heath government and that they had 'frustrated the more socialist policies' of the Labour government elected in 1974.

> Civil servants at the Department of Industry have been culpable in frustrating . . . interventionist industrial policies . . . In this case political bias may have played a part. The result is that instead of an industrial strategy we have a series of industrial problems. The Department of Trade contains civil servants who are steeped in nineteenth century Board of Trade attitudes . . . Civil servants . . . are also known to be hostile to any meaningful form of industrial democracy although it is Labour Party policy . . . The Home Office, the graveyard of free-thinking since the days of Lord Sidmouth early in the nineteenth century, is stuffed with reactionaries ruthlessly pursuing their own reactionary policies . . . Some Foreign Office officials interpret being a good European as being synonymous with selling out British interests. The Vichy mentality which undoubtedly exists in some parts of our Foreign Office establishment does not to the best of our knowledge and belief reflect the views of Her Majesty's Ministers.

The Treasury, apparently, had 'messed up everything over the past 25 years'.[12]

Departments do have traditional positions on policy. In the 1850s George Arbuthnot, a leading civil servant, wrote that 'the humble and useful duty' of officials was to become 'depositories of departmental tradition' so as 'to keep the current business in due course'. Taking up this theme in the 1950s, Sir Edward Bridges said that 'there has been built up in every department a store of knowledge and experience in the subjects handled, something which eventually takes shape as a practical philosophy, or may merit the title of a departmental point of view'. Bridges believed that 'these departmental philosophies are of the essence of a civil servant's work'. When policy was being framed, it was 'the duty of a civil servant to give his Minister the fullest benefit of the storehouse of departmental experience; and to let the waves of the practical philosophy wash against ideas put forward by his ministerial master'. Writing in 1938, Laski had thought it obvious that 'every department worth its salt has a policy of its own; a body of able men cannot long have direction of an administrative process without seeking to define the latitude and longitude of that direction'. Laski was as unenthusiastic as the English Committee's Minority had been about the particular 'departmental philosophies' of the Treasury, the Foreign Office, the Home Office and the Board of Trade. He found it easy to see how such 'philosophies' were imposed upon 'lay' ministers. However, unlike other critics, Laski pointed to the obvious solution under the parliamentary system. This was that the political parties should prepare properly for governing, so that they did not have 'to trust to the ingenuity of the Civil Service to improvise a policy after office has been taken'. For 'the proper direction of the departments' by the government, its programme had to be more than ' declaration of intentions, a pious hope of fulfilments sought for'. It had to have 'solid investigation' behind it. Laski recognized that 'this predicates, of course, for the modern political party something like a Civil Service of its own. It must have at its disposal not merely men who can write well sounding propaganda leaflets.' One notes that forty-five years later, one of Sir John Hoskyns's prescriptions for reform was 'taxpayer support for the political parties, so that they can maintain shadow teams of officials' who would then accompany the parties into office.[13]

Governments can govern in the British system. Indeed, the higher civil service is primarily organized in support of ministerial responsibility. The perennial difficulty has been that the parties and the ministers drawn from them are normally unprepared to play their role in governing. Hence, largely by default, higher civil servants are thrust into the position of a 'permanent government', for which their experience as a particular type of subordinate does not usually fit them. While, naturally, not being averse to developments which benefit it, the higher civil service provides a framework that underpins the status quo. In the absence of coherent political initiatives to change that, the civil servants are bound to proceed along familiar lines. Thus, departmental traditions persist and even an overall strategy of some kind may emerge – of 'the common ground' variety noted later – in the absence of a government strategy. A succession of weak governments did seem to lead to some higher civil servants forgetting their subordinate station, and the reassertion of effective political control after 1979 met with a measure of opposition. Nevertheless, the general experience of the first Thatcher government served to emphasize the subordinate position of the higher civil service.

Civil service 'obstruction' would be bound to be an inadequate explanation for the 'failure' of successive recent British governments. That such an explanation is so widely subscribed to partly reflects the tendency of British politics to be conducted and discussed as if Britain still had the relative political and economic power in the world that she enjoyed before 1914. Parties still talk of 'coming to power', whereas, if successful in obtaining what is better described as office, responsibilities are what they inherit. This is not to say that well-prepared and/or determined governments can never implement their programmes. It is to suggest that the British political debate (and that about the civil service too) might be healthier, even marginally more honest, if the multiplicity of constraints upon British governments were more widely acknowledged. That, for instance, Britain did not pursue 'a socialist foreign policy' after 1945 was not largely explained, as Laski thought, by excessive Foreign Office influence over Ernest Bevin. A more likely explanation was that Britain's wartime exertions had left her in a poor position to pursue an independent foreign policy of any kind. The accusation that the Foreign Office displays a 'Vichy mentality' of which ministers are not guilty requires substantiation. In the infamous case of the Foreign Office's involvement at the end of the war in the enforced repatriation to the Soviet Union – and, hence, to their deaths – of thousands of people who were not even that country's citizens, there is no doubt about the political responsibility of Sir Anthony Eden and Harold Macmillan. Pusillanimous attitudes towards the Soviet Union, excessive Atlanticism, faith in the benefits of being 'a good European' – what the 'Vichy mentality' means presumably – if and when present have not been the Foreign Office's monopoly. It was the exceptional British politician in the 1970s, for instance, who did not believe in *détente* with the Soviet Union. Churchill as 'Former Naval Person' established a deferential 'special relationship' with the USA which such as Macmillan zestfully pursued. The Foreign Office – led by Eden as Foreign Secretary – was hostile to closer ties with continental Europe at that stage in the 1950s when British prestige was still high. There is a certain irony in the fact that eventual membership of the EEC, obtained on unfavorable terms, gave what is now the Foreign and Commonwealth Office unprecedented formal rights to be consulted about the policies of domestic departments where their work has a 'European' dimension. While there is a bureaucratic network in Brussels itself, which has the appearance of a 'mandarin's paradise', there is no definite evidence that the British element is outside political control. [14] While normally open to political correction, the occupational disease of British diplomacy does seem to be the seeking of 'good relations' with other countries at almost any price. In 1956, though, it was not a professional diplomat, but – if one recent account is accurate – Sir Norman Brook, the head of the home civil service, who took this attitude to the point of gross disloyalty when he communicated the Eden government's confidential plans for the Suez venture – of which he disapproved – to the Americans through the intelligence network. [15]

The notion that the domestic policies of successive postwar governments have been largely dictated by the civil service seems difficult to sustain, and the responsibility of the parties for their performance in office seems clear. A sea change took place in British politics in the 1940s when the managed economy welfare state was established. Politicians of all colours promised that the new order would mean that real incomes would increase perennially, price stability would be attained, full employment would be sustained and the social services would be continually expanded. The crucial difference with the 1906 dispensation was that Keynes had deposed Marshall as 'authority' in economics which, combined with the effects of two total wars in a generation, in practice meant that traditional attitudes towards the containment of public expenditure were undermined. The money was always supposed to be there – for a start, to implement the Beveridge Plan. The Coalition government's commitment of its peacetime successors to the maintenance of 'a high and stable level of employment without sacrificing the essential liberties of a free society' was a substantial undertaking especially for a country so heavily dependent on external trade. Keynesianism was a classic example of politicians having an exaggerated belief in the extent to which Britain could act independently. In 1951 Hugh Gaitskell, Labour's Chancellor of the Exchequer, defined full employment in terms of 3 per cent unemployment or less, emphasizing that enlightened policies would ensure less. His Tory successor, R. A. Butler, proceeded on the same assumptions. Nobody has yet offered a convincing explanation of why Britain enjoyed full employment on the 'Butskell' scale for so long as she did: but the pursuit of supposedly enlightened Keynesian macroeconomic management seems unlikely to have been the decisive factor. While it had been damaged, the British economy was relatively well placed in 1945 compared with those of her defeated foes and some of her former allies. This advantage was lost, but it took time, and certainly for a decade Britain still had a relatively quiescent labour force with unambitious consumption demands and a moderately led trade union movement which did not press its market advantage. Such domestic factors, though, pale in importance when compared with the sustained boom in international trade – in which Britain shared – that prospered under the Pax Americana and cheap energy until the effects of the Vietnam War and the 1973 oil crisis brought it to a halt. Long before this, the end of the Butler boom in 1955 had signalled that whatever the merits of the British managed economy welfare state, it was not an economic and social order that would enable Britain to keep material pace with her main rivals. There were then three main alternatives. One was the socialist alternative which in Marxist countries, thus far, involved universal state ownership of the means of production, distribution and exchange, rationing, and the direction of labour. A second course was the social market approach – to emphasize the role of private enterprise more, on West German lines. These approaches appealed neither to the Tory government of Macmillan nor the Labour leadership of the time. Effectively, they chose the third course which was to proceed as if there was nothing essentially wrong. Anthony Crosland gave this approach some thin intellectual clothes. The Macmillan government went down the path of economic planning and incomes policy. It also began the fashion for institutional change. This had the logic to it that, given that the ends pursued were all supposed to be attainable together, because they were not being so attained it seemed to follow that the means – the machinery of government and the men who permanently manned its core – had to be at fault. So, whereas it had seemed quixotic when, in 1954, W. A. Robson had revived the Laski reform programme as his way of celebrating the Trevelyan–Northcote Report's centenary, from the latter half of the 1950s onwards attacks on the Treasury and the civil service were commonplace. This was the road to Fulton.[16]

While the civil service has its own interests in maintaining, preferably expanding, the bureaucracy and in avoiding the disruptions caused by discontinuities in policy, there was more to the 'failures' of successive governments than civil service obstruction. With an 'economic miracle' not being forthcoming, what was then bound to be an excessively ambitious role expected of governments under the managed economy welfare state doomed them to 'failure' anyway. The Benn thesis, primarily blaming the civil service, was less perceptive than Laski's in that it ignored the deficiencies of party. According to Benn, 'the bold challenge of the 1964 Labour Government's "new Britain" manifesto was gradually absorbed and finally defused by 20th July 1966, when the Treasury persuaded the then Chancellor to insist upon a package of economic measures that killed the National Plan and instituted a statutory pay policy'. The fact was that in 'thirteen wasted years' in Opposition between 1951 and 1964, the Labour Party had not drawn up contingency plans for ameliorating the effects on such economic strategy as it had of the runs on sterling which were bound to punctuate its next period of office. That the Wilson governments had to rely on the Treasury to fill the gap was the Labour Party's own responsibility. The 'new Britain' was never more than a slogan. The party of planning has never possessed detailed, practicable plans for office. The translation of the Short Programme, which Laski had talked about, into the 1945 nationalization programme primarily resulted from Conference pressure. There were no plans, even for coal nationalization. So the civil servants had to do the work. The 1965 National Plan was an inflated version of the Neddy Plan of 1963, lacking even a revision mechanism. It could never be more than 'a declaration of intentions'. Contrary to the Benn version, Labour has never had a manifesto 'into which an enormous amount of detailed work has gone'. This is also true of the Conservatives. The Conservative Research Department has no serious counterpart on the Labour side: but in its golden age under R. A. Butler after 1945 its role was concentrated on convincing the electorate that the Tories could be trusted to run the managed economy welfare state. When rethinking was needed after 1955 it was not forthcoming, and the preparations for office made after 1964 in Opposition – with the exception of Sir Arthur Cockfield's tax plans – seem well described by Lord Boyle as superficial. In Benn's opinion, the civil service was again to blame 'when the 1970 Conservative Government was driven off its commitment to the free market philosophy developed at Selsdon Park and the then Prime Minister was persuaded to do a U turn which took him back to the policies Macmillan had developed from 1962 to 1963, and that Wilson had been persuaded to follow from 1966 to 1970'. As Edward Heath was a Macmillanite anyway he might not have taken much persuading, doubtful thought it must be that any took place. The Boyle view that Heath was never wedded to the Selsdon philosophy and only adopted it from a position of weakness as Leader of the Opposition seems more credible. Fear of the electoral consequences of presiding over a combination of rising prices and unemployment was probably a more potent reason for the Heath government's U-turn than any civil service pressure. Undaunted, Benn blamed the service again when 'after the referendum in 1975 – the Labour Government was persuaded to abandon its 1974 manifesto and to return to the policies of 1972–74, as pursued by Mr Heath'. Another way of looking at this is that, having had the EEC referendum thrust upon him, Harold Wilson, with the aid of the electorate, took the opportunity to inflict a signal defeat on those in the party like Benn and in the unions who claimed a special right to speak for the mass of the people. Only then, could the Labour government safely drop its pretence that remedial economic measures were not needed in the wake of the oil crisis.[17]

Such civil service obstruction as there was supposed to be to Mr Benn's attempts to translate Labour's manifesto commitments into practice, when he was Secretary of State for Industry and then for Energy between 1974 and 1979, seem less important than the opposition presented by the majority of the Labour Cabinet. Mr Benn's overriding problem – as he himself recorded – was well summed up by Sir Antony Part, his permanent secretary at the Department of Industry, when he said that the secretary of state was a 'radical Minister in a non-radical Government'. Both Benn and Brian Sedgemore believed that prime ministers as well as higher civil servants act 'unconstitutionally'; but, should it exist, even when combined, such behaviour by the former diminished the importance of the latter. Sedgemore's documentation of civil service obstruction of Mr Benn is difficult to examine because the officials themselves have not chosen to reply fully. On the matter, though, of workers' co-operatives it can be said that any lack of enthusiasm on the part of the civil servants was at least matched in the Cabinet. Peter Carey, as second permanent secretary in the Department of Industry, did take an unusual step in 1975 when – as accounting officer responsible for public expenditure under the Industry Act – he made a written objection to the provision of £3·9 million to the Kirkby co-operative. Sedgemore pointed out that the sum concerned was trifling compared with the hundreds of millions of pounds lost by Rolls-Royce and on the Concorde project. This was so, but there was no obvious disagreement within the government on the latter forms of expenditure, whereas co-operatives were contentious. That the sum involved was small would not have saved Carey from possible censure by the Public Accounts Committee which deals with both large and small sums and, indeed, may find the latter easier to comprehend. Sir Anthony Part limited himself to the later observation about ministers that 'most experienced practitioners of my acquaintance do not subscribe to the idea that their departments are somehow out to frustrate them, still less that there is some kind of inter-departmental conspiracy among officials to put a brake on change. For obvious human reasons civil servants prefer to work for Ministers with minds of their own and who are likely to succeed. The legend of the lonely Minister surrounded by scheming bureaucrats is usually put about by weak Ministers.'[18]

The notions that the civil service has come to act as if it was 'an estate of the realm with a policy of its own', and that higher civil servants have come to think of themselves as 'guardians and trustees of national continuity', were dismissed by Part. Yet, he has said that 'the Civil Service always hopes that it's influencing Ministers towards the common ground. Now that's not to say influencing them towards some piece of ground which the Civil Service has itself constructed; it is the Civil Service trying to have a sense of what can succeed for Britain, and trying to exercise its influence on Ministers to try to see that they do capture the common ground with their ideas, from whatever origin they start.' This 'common ground' was not 'the centre' because that was 'literally half-way between the two poles, while the common ground is the ground on which, or to which the majority of people can be persuaded to move. You have to remember that in recent times neither of the main political parties has been elected by a majority of the electorate.' Unlike the higher civil service, though, those political parties did present themselves to the electorate and, under the electoral system, that party which won the most seats could expect to have the authority to form the government and to have the opportunity to implement its programme. That the civil service has the right to guide governments towards 'the common ground' seems questionable. What is this 'common ground' to consist of? In the days of the Keynesian consensus the agenda could be fairly easily established: but the limitations of Croslandism were exposed by the record of the Wilson governments of 1964–70, and the effects of the oil crisis and the manner of the collapse of the Heath government ensured the radicalization of British politics. Sir John Hoskyns was correct in saying that the civil service has no legitimate role in acting as constitutional ballast. If polarisation is a fact of political life then seeking 'the common ground' is not an a-political position. There is survey evidence that, in general, Conservative policy attitudes commended wide support outside the ranks of Tory voters in 1979. If there was a 'common ground' the Conservative government elected then seemed to be occupying much of it. Yet, there was discord between that government and some of its leading officials. In the central area of economic policy the Thatcher government did not accept what Sir William Armstrong had called the Treasury's neo-Keynesian framework of economic thinking. When that government sought to reconsider its financial commitments in the area of social provision a series of leaks of confidential documents occurred. Indeed, at times, the Labour Party's campaign in the 1983 election relied heavily on such material. After the Conservative victory, Sir Robert Armstrong, the head of the home civil service, in a letter to all forty permanent secretaries which was itself leaked, wrote that higher civil servants must have been the main source of the leaks which could only have been deliberately perpetrated with the object of embarrassing the Tory government. Sir Robert said that such behaviour displayed a corrupt sense of values. Those civil servants who could not act loyally towards the government of the day should resign. Only those with a taste for casuistry could easily quarrel with that position. Civil service affection for the Keynesian consensus – 'the common ground' in disguise – was not necessarily disinterested. The scale of machinery of government needed to sustain that consensus provided higher civil servants with generous opportunities for advancement and for interesting work – 'fine tuning' the economy, and so forth. Cutting back on the role of the state, as the Heath government was initially committed to doing, and which the Thatcher government made a more sustained effort to do, threatens those arrangements. That the civil service has a self-interest to defend was made clear appropriately enough by the then leader of its union movement, W. L. Kendall, in 1980 when he said that in cutting it Mrs Thatcher risked politicizing the service, as if the government was acting excessively in fulfilling this manifesto commitment. Overt political activity by civil servants remains restricted by rules laid down in 1953: but during the 1983 election campaign the Council of Civil Service Unions was still free to distribute material to the memberships concerned which pointed to Labour as the party that would do most to defend the immediate interests of civil servants.[19] If a body as large as the civil service, even the higher civil service, can be seriously said to have a political bias, it seems most likely to be one favouring parties which more naturally look for bureaucratic solutions to political problems and which are given to expanding the service and to protecting, even advancing, its privileges, not least in terms of pay and conditions.

Changing Directions for the Higher Civil Service?
The resistance which the Thatcher government felt that it experienced was what caused the Prime Minister's former adviser, Sir John Hoskyns, to call for the reform of the higher civil service. Sir John said that the first Thatcher government had brought the nation's finances under proper control for the first time in twenty-five years: but, with Britain fighting for nothing less than survival as an advanced industrial country, that still left the challenge of establishing a flourishing, internationally competitive economy. Radical change in the Westminster–Whitehall arrangements was required. First, Westminster having the character of a university debating society, the Prime Minister should no longer be restricted to selecting ministers from the small pool of career politicians there – a pool of talent insufficient to sustain a single international company. Under the existing system, professional politicians became amateur ministers of generally low calibre, changing jobs too frequently and having an appalling workload, poor facilities and irrelevant experience. Secondly,

Whitehall must be organized for strategy and innovation, as well as for day-to-day political survival. Most postwar governments had, like hamsters, gone round and round in a strategic box too small to contain any solutions. A more positive approach was now required from Whitehall and businessmen should be brought in to provide it, working in an atmosphere of open government. As noted before, Sir John wanted the state financing of political parties to enable these appointees to prepare for their tasks and he also wanted civil service heads to roll. 'We need to replace a large number of senior civil servants with politically appointed officials on contracts, at proper market rates, so that experienced top quality people would be available', Sir John said. 'They might number between ten and twenty per department. Some of them would fill senior positions in the department. Others might work as policy advisers to the Cabinet Minister concerned. There is no reason why, in some cases, the Permanent Secretary should not be an outsider, with a career official as Second Permanent Secretary responsible for the day-to-day running of the department.'[20]

With the economic orthodoxy having returned to that of the 1920s, it is scarcely surprising that the belief that businessmen would do a better job in Whitehall than the 'faceless bureaucrats' should enjoy a revival too. In this respect what, for example, Sir Stephen Demetriadi was writing in 1921, Sir John Hoskyns was expounding sixty years later. While since the 1964 Labour government the use of political appointees as advisers – sometimes highly placed – has become more familiar, the total numbers have remained small – a maximum of about thirty overall at a time – so that the scale of the Hoskyns influx would be a departure from established British administrative practice. Of course, this is the intention. American experience seems instructive. The Americans are used to a system of 'in-and-outers' in the federal civil service, and have a society more attuned to career mobility generally and one in which private business has more prestige than in Britain and presumably attracts proportionately more talent and, hence, has relatively more of it to spare. Yet, one recent comprehensive survey of political appointees in the American federal bureaucracy – most of whom were originally drawn from the private sector – found their performance in office to be so unimpressive that the scholar concerned ended up calling for something resembling the Fisher-style administrative class to be established there. In 1955 the second Hoover Commission had recommended the creation of a senior civil service on similar lines. It even seems debatable whether or not the American spoils system ensures the political responsiveness within the bureaucracy that would be its most convincing defence. The Hoskyns arrangements might not degenerate into a spoils system – but they do encourage scepticism about their practicability. In sentimental moments the British civil service at least used to be said to be 'second to none' (although less often since the EEC negotiations of 1961–3 emphasized the professionalism of that of the French). To judge from the results achieved, admittedly in relation to what may be harsher competition, British private sector management appears to be 'second to many' in overall quality. This judgement may be severe: but it does seem likely that British private companies simply do not have the pool of talent available to easily release very able people on the Hoskyns scale to serve political parties and then in Whitehall. In a relatively immobile society like Britain's, career considerations might make the ambitious reluctant to move too. The teams of businessmen used for Rayner rationalization exercises by both the Heath and Thatcher governments were small ones. Nothing on the Hoskyns lines seems envisaged, at least as yet. There was an emphasis on more interchange with, and more permanent recruitment from, industry and commerce in a Management and Personnel Office document published in 1983, but not, it was stressed, on a scale which would interfere with the maintenance of a career service.[21]

The difficulty persists, though, that in the recent past a career higher civil service has been found wanting by both Conservative and Labour governments – if not always for disinterested reasons – and, now, not everybody seems to be as complacent as the Webbs were in 1920 about what they saw as the 'fact' that 'the government of Great Britain is . . . carried on, not by the Cabinet, nor even by individual Ministers, but by the Civil Service'. Not even the Webbs in their *Constitution for the Socialist Commonwealth of Great Britain* spelled out what a 'socialist Civil Service' would look like. Indeed, at one point, the Webbs implicitly endorsed the Fisher mobile administrator. Later thinking among socialists tended to be of the Laski–Robson reform variety. The Labour Party's evidence to Fulton favouring French-style ministerial *cabinets* was a departure from its tradition of largely negative criticism. As we have seen, Tony Benn thought that the power of the higher civil service was too great – 'they do think that they are the ultimate government of the country and that Ministers may come and go, but in them resides the ultimate responsibility'. Nevertheless, although Benn believed that they acted 'unconstitutionally' he still favoured a 'professional' service. Quite how this was supposed to be prevented from acting as a 'permanent government' in the manner resented was not convincingly shown. A Freedom of Information Act, as Benn proposed, might well not make that much difference. Official

Secrets legislation does not extend to local government, but decision-making there tends to be secretive. Of a famed 'open' system of central government, we learn that

> the main area of political life is hidden in Sweden, as elsewhere. No publicity rule can give access to the political basis behind a decision, the political thinking and calculations . . . Once the political decision as to the direction which is to be taken has been made, then the details of how best to implement this decision are much more open to view, especially the factual basis used by the Government to justify its decisions. The irony, however, is that because of the nature of Swedish politics, the availability of information does not lead to a lively political debate.

The nature of British politics differs, not least through being more competitive, and it seems likely that confidentiality in the form of unrecorded discussions, literally kitchen Cabinets if necessary, would persist whatever the legislation.[22]

The most important factor leading to governments becoming heavily dependent on the higher civil service remains the unwillingness or inability of British political parties to prepare for office. Richard Crossman recognized early on about the Labour Cabinet of 1964 that 'what we lacked was any comprehensive, thoroughly thought-out Government strategy. The policies are being thrown together.' By 1967, according to Crossman, such was the closeness of the relationship between the Prime Minister and the Secretary of the Cabinet that the Labour government had become 'a Wilson–Burke Trend axis'. If this was the case, the responsibility was that of Wilson and the government. Trend should have been treated as a subordinate. The Heath government, too, ended up in a position of excessive dependency. As it sank towards defeat, a meeting involving higher civil servants was held at Downing Street, of which the Prime Minister's political secretary, Douglas Hurd, later wrote:

> It should have provided a chance for that clear-headed analysis of the options before the Government, which was by then badly needed. Instead there was silence on the big issues and a confused, bitty discussion of trivial tactical points. I felt critical of the senior civil servants present, whose duty it should have been to force the discussion into some coherent channel. This was the third and final occasion when I felt that at a crucial moment they fell below what was required . . . No one who was present at any of these three meetings could believe that the Civil Service runs the country.

But, then, it is not supposed to. If the Heath government had lost its way, that was its responsibility. The relationship which that government came to have with Sir William Armstrong, the head of the home civil service, was another indication of excessive dependency. According to Sir Leo Pliatsky, Sir William, having soon found his duties at the CSD unexciting, longed to be involved in economic policy making again as he had been at the Treasury. Having established a rapport with the Prime Minister, Armstrong proceeded to act as Heath's right-hand man in negotiations with the trade unions over incomes policy. Armstrong came to be seen as 'the deputy Prime Minister'. When Heath lost office, Armstrong, having been so closely linked with the Conservative government, had little choice about resigning several months later.[23]

Lack of preparation renders ministers over-dependent on their officials too. Crossman anticipated this. Before taking office he wrote that 'a Minister must normally be content with the role of public relations officer to his department, unless the Prime Minister appointed him with the express purpose of carrying out reforms'. In 1964 Crossman suddenly found that he was 'not to be Secretary of State for Education but Minister of Housing. About this job I knew virtually nothing. Indeed the only preparations I had made which were of any use were those that concerned my diary.' At the Ministry of Housing, Crossman found himself 'floating on the most comfortable support'. This he appeared to need, for nothing in his life as an academic, journalist, or MP seemed to have prepared him to be a minister of the Crown. At least when at Housing, Crossman could not hope to be more than a 'public relations officer'. The House of Commons increasingly seems to attract Crossman's type, with no experience of industry or commerce. Those who value that kind of experience are likely to see the Commons as providing a poor source of ministerial talent: but bringing in outsiders, as Sir John Hoskyns proposed, rarely works well in peacetime. Even the very able Ernest Bevin never quite seemed to come to grips with his parliamentary duties and, more recently, Frank Cousins and John Davies fared similarly. The Hoskyns notion of an alternative higher civil service waiting in the wings would probably not work on grounds of lack of suitable personnel in the numbers required: but state funding of party policy research, if only on a pound for pound basis, might be practicable. There have been institutional attempts to fill the policy 'gap' in British central government which follows from the parties' inadequacies. The Heath government introduced the Central Policy Review Staff (CPRS), which for a time acted as if it was a surrogate for an effective Cabinet. The Fulton Report proposed that government departments should establish policy planning units. Some departments already had them (that of the Board of Customs and Excise dated from 1922), and now almost all departments from the Treasury downwards do. Of course, the findings of policy planning units cannot commit ministers, and they may serve to consolidate the departmental traditions which some ministers resent. The proliferation of planning units within departments was given by the Thatcher government as one reason why it felt able to dispense with the CPRS in 1983.[24]

Within the framework set by the requirements of British parliamentary democracy, it is open to established governments to change the higher civil service to its liking. Such a service composed of 'outsiders' would still be vulnerable to ministers saying 'why wasn't I told' and likely to act with caution on behalf of their politically exposed parliamentary heads. Even relatively recently, ministers, themselves given to playing 'musical chairs' between departments, in practice, have not always looked with disfavour on the Fisher-type generalist. In 1975, for instance, when Barbara Castle was Secretary of State for Social Services, the then head of the home civil service suggested that Sir Patrick Nairne should become her permanent under secretary at the DHSS. 'David Owen [her Minister of State] first mentioned him to me', Mrs Castle recorded, 'having formed a very high opinion of him when Nairne was Denis's Private Secretary at Defence. Denis [Healey] too raves about him.' Sir Patrick Nairne's career had been largely spent in the defence area – apart from a spell in the Cabinet Office – and he later said that his transfer to the DHSS involved some anxious reading up of the subject matter: 'I knew nothing about the Health Service and nothing about the social services at all.' Mrs Castle found Nairne to be 'an excellent civil servant.'[25] Should governments want this type of policy adviser, the higher civil service will oblige, with a career pattern involving frequent changes between not necessarily related jobs to match. The first Thatcher government's dissatisfaction with the higher civil service which it had inherited, and with that service acting as if it was a 'permanent government', was evident from the outset. The Rayner exercises, the MINIS approach, the chopping back of the service's career ladder and the elimination of the CSD (involving as it did the early retirement of the head of the home civil service) all served to emphasize the determination of that particular Conservative government to get its way. If the balance of power between politicians and the higher bureaucracy needed to be redressed after a succession of ineffectual governments, then, despite, it seems, some opposition, even disloyalty, the first Thatcher government asserted the supremacy of the politician as part of its strategy for attempting to bring the national finances under control. The intention to retain a career civil service was stated, but the managerial issues that involved themselves presented problems the resolution of which has been on the reformers' agenda for decades.

References

1   Sir E. E. Bridges, *Portrait of a Profession* (London, 1950), p. 19; Sir D. Wass, 'The public service in modern society', *Public Administration*, vol. 61 (1983), pp. 7–20.

2   *Report of the Committee on the Civil Service* (Fulton Report), Cmnd 3638 (1968), paras 1, 15; A. L. Lowell, *The Government of England*, Vol. I (London, 1908), pp. 173, 182.

3   *Statement Submitted by the Permanent Secretary to the Treasury to the Royal Commission on the Civil Service* (1930), p. 1267; *Report on the Organization of the Permanent Civil Service* (Trevelyan–Northcote Report) (1853), pp. 3–23; G. K. Fry, *Statesmen in Disguise* (London, 1969), pp. 36–66.

4   ibid., pp. 52–4; Sir H. P. Hamilton, 'Sir Warren Fisher and the public service', *Public Administration*, vol. 29 (1951), pp. 3–38; *Tomlin Evidence*, p. 1269, qq. 18556, 18787, 18809; G. C. Peden, 'Sir Warren Fisher and British rearmament against Germany', *English Historical Review*, vol. 94 (1979), pp. 29–47. The writer owes the information about Fisher's attempt to replace Vansittart to D. J. Dilks, author of a forthcoming biography of Neville Chamberlain.

5   H. E. Dale, *The Higher Civil Service of Great Britain* (London, 1941), p. 220; C. H. Sisson, *The Spirit of British Administration*, 2nd edn (London, 1966), p. 13.

6   *Second Report from the Select Committee on the Parliamentary Commissioner for Administration*, HC 350 (1967–8), para. 24; E. C. S. Wade and G. C. Philips, *Constitutional and Administrative Law*, 9th edn (London, 1977), ed. A. W. Bradley, pp. 105–7; G. K. Fry, 'Thoughts on the present state of the convention of ministerial responsibility', *Parliamentary Affairs*, vol. 23 (1969–70), pp. 10–20; G. K. Fry, 'The Sachsenhausen concentration camp case and the convention of ministerial responsibility', *Public Law* (1970), pp. 336–57.

7   E. Dell in W. Rodgers *et al.*, *Policy and Practice. The Experience of Government* (London, 1980), p. 47; S. E. Finer, 'The individual responsibility of ministers', *Public Administration*, vol. 34 (1956), pp. 377–96.

8   Dale, *Higher Civil Service*, p. 213; *David Dimbleby in Conversation with Sir John Hoskyns*, BBC 1 Television, 7 December 1982.

9   T. Benn in Rodgers *et al.*, *Policy and Practice*, pp. 57–78; T. Benn, *Arguments for Democracy* (London, 1981), pp. 47–67; *Eleventh Report from the Expenditure Committee. The Civil Service* (English Report), HC 535–I (1976), pp. lxiii–lxv, lxxviii–lxxxiii.

10   G. W. E. Russell, *Collections and Recollections* (London, 1903), pp. 332–3; Dale, *Higher Civil Service*, p. 107; H. J. Laski, *Parliamentary Government in England* (London, 1938), pp. 84, 315–22; H. J. Laski, 'Introduction', in J. P. W. Mallalieu, *Passed to You Please* (London, 1942), pp. 6–16; M. Williams, *Inside Number Ten* (London, 1972), pp. 27, 28, 344–59; *The Civil Service*, vol. 3, pt 2. *Surveys and Investigations. Evidence submitted to the Committee under the Chairmanship of Lord Fulton 1966–68*, p. 9; M. Falkender, *Downing Street in Perspective* (London, 1983), pp. 260–3.

11   Sir G. Jackson, *Concorde Diplomacy* (London, 1981), pp. 79–80.

12   Benn, *Arguments for Democracy*, pp. 50, 52; English Report, pp. lxxx–lxxxi.

13   Sir E. E. Bridges, 'The reforms of 1854 in retrospect', *Political Quarterly*, vol. 25 (1954), p. 322; Bridges, *Portrait of a Profession*, pp. 15–17; Laski, *Parliamentary Government*, pp. 296–300, 336–8; Sir J. Hoskyns, 'Whitehall and Westminster: an outsider's view', *Parliamentary Affairs*, vol. 36 (1983), p. 146.

14   The best account of the EEC arrangements remains H. Wallace, W. Wallace and C. Webb

(eds), *Policy-Making in the European Communities* (London, 1977); and of British involvement in the British bureaucracy that of H. Young and A. Sloman, *No, Minister. An Inquiry into the Civil Service* (London, 1982), pp. 73–85.

15 A Verrier, *Through the Looking Glass* (London, 1983), pp. 142–8, 150–3. The Foreign Office's Sir Patrick Dean (just) stopped short of revealing all of what he knew to the CIA's link man in London at the time, C. L. Cooper (see the latter's *The Lion's Last Roar*, New York, 1978, p. 159).

16 *Employment Policy*, Cmnd 6527 (1944), para. 87; A. J. Deacon in B. Showler and A. Sinfield (eds), *The Workless State* (Oxford, 1981), p. 67; G. K. Fry, *The Administrative 'Revolution' in Whitehall* (London, 1981), pp. 3–35; W. A. Robson, 'The civil service and its critics', *Political Quarterly*, vol. 25 (1954), pp. 299–307.

17 T. Benn in Rodgers *et al., Policy and Practice*, p. 62; Benn, *Arguments for Democracy*, p. 52; interview with Lord Boyle, 26 April 1977.

18 Young and Sloman, *No, Minister*, pp. 29–30; B. Sedgemore, *The Secret Constitution* (London, 1980), pp. 88–147; Sir A. Part, 'Change-makers of Whitehall', *Listener*, 31 July 1980, p. 132.

19 ibid., pp. 130–1; D. Jessel, 'Mandarins and ministers', *Listener*, 11 December 1980, p. 775; *David Dimbleby in Conversation with Sir John Hoskyns*, BBC 1 Television, 7 December 1982; *Guardian*, 30 May 1983, 31 August 1983; *The Times*, 15 November 1976, 12 August 1980. *The Political Activities of Civil Servants*, Cmd 8783 (1953) laid down the rules which still govern that area. The Conservative hold on 'the common ground' by 1979 was documented by M. Harrop in R. M. Worcester and M. Harrop (eds.), *Political Communications* (London, 1982), pp. 152–63; I. Crewe in D. Kavanagh (ed.), *The Politics of the Labour Party* (London, 1982), pp. 9–49; B. Sarlvik and I. Crewe, *Decade of Dealignment* (London, 1983), pp. 119–280.

20 Sir J. Hoskyns, 'Whitehall and Westminster: an outsider's view', *Parliamentary Affairs*, vol. 36 (1983), pp. 137–47; Sir J. Hoskyns, 'Strip down the state machine and start again', *The Times*, 16 February 1983; *Daily Telegraph*, 29 September 1983; Sir J. Hoskyns, 'How to galvanise the moribund Establishment which rules Britain', *Guardian*, 30 September 1983.

21 Sir S. Demetriadi, *Inside a Government Office* (London, 1921) and *A Reform for the Civil Service* (London, 1921); W. S. Sayre in A. J. Junz (ed.), *Present Trends in American National Government* (London, 1960), pp. 112–25; H. Heclo, *A Government of Strangers* (Washington DC, 1977), pp. 249–53; C. Peters and M. Nelson (eds) *The Culture of Bureaucracy* (New York, 1979), pp. 263–7; M. Nelson, 'A short ironic history of American national bureaucracy', *Journal of Politics*, vol. 44 (1982), pp. 747–78; Management and Personnel Office (MPO), *Civil Service Management Development in the 1980s* (1983), paras 18–21.

22 S. and B. Webb, *A Constitution for the Socialist Commonwealth of Great Britain* (London, 1920), pp. 66–70, 175–6; The Civil Service, vol. 5, pt 2. *Proposals and Opinions. Parts 3 and 4. Organisations and Individuals. Evidence submitted to the Committee under the Chairmanship of Lord Fulton 1966–68*, pp. 665–6; Young and Sloman, *No, Minister*, pp. 94–5; K. G. Robertson, *Public Secrets* (London, 1982), pp. 178–9.

23 R. H. S. Crossman, *The Diaries of a Cabinet Minister*, Vol. 1 (London, 1975), p. 39, and Vol. 2 (London, 1976), p. 296; D. Hurd, *An End to Promises* (London, 1979), pp. 117–18; Sir L. Pliatsky, *Getting and Spending* (Oxford, 1982), pp. 108–9, 116, 123.

24 R. H. S. Crossman, 'Introduction' in W. Bagehot, *The English Constitution* (London, 1963 edn), p. 51; Crossman, *Diaries*, Vol. 1, pp. 12, 31; Fulton Report, pp. 57–61; G. K. Fry, 'Policy planning units in British central government departments', *Public Administration*, vol. 50 (1972), pp. 139–55; J. H. Macdonald and G. K. Fry, 'Policy planning units – ten years on', *Public Administration*, vol. 58 (1980), pp. 421–37; *The Times*, 17 June 1983.

25 B. Castle, *The Castle Diaries 1974–76* (London, 1980), pp. 467, 733; *The Times*, 17 July 1981.

3 Managerial Issues in the Changing Civil Service

1 Structure, Direct-Entry Recruitment and Post-Entry Training

With few of the government departments they manned escaping merger and/or renaming from the early 1960s onwards, it was always unlikely that the structure of the non-industrial civil service, and its direct-entry recruitment and post-entry training arrangements, would elude similar reformist attention. The Fulton Committee, of course, provided the main focus of such attention in relation to the home civil service, but that part of the civil service concerned with overseas representation attracted no less than three external inquiries at various points in Britain's international decline: the Plowden Committee of 1962–3, the Duncan Committee of 1968–9 and that conducted by the Central Policy Review Staff (CPRS) in 1976–7. Plowden recommended the merger of the foreign service, the commonwealth service, and the trade commissioner service into a diplomatic service which was established in 1965. Plowden confined itself to gentle criticism, Duncan and the CPRS, reviewing overseas representation in less expansive times, chose to be more forceful. However expressed, their critique of the diplomatic service was predictable. It was well summarized by the authors of the 1943 reforms of the foreign service:

> that it is recruited from too small a circle, that it tends to represent the interests of certain sections of the nation rather than those of the country as a whole, that its members lead too sheltered a life, that they have insufficient understanding of economic and social questions, that the extent of their experience is too small to enable them properly to understand many of the problems with which they ought to deal, and that the range of their contacts is too limited to allow them to acquire more than a relatively narrow acquaintance with the foreign peoples amongst whom they live.

The cost of diplomatic entertaining and of the general upkeep of diplomatic missions and the grand scale of some of the buildings are other stock sources of criticism. The preference which the diplomatic service is said to give to its political work in relation to its commercial work is another common target. The main ingredients having been similarly supplied by Laski and Robson long before, the diet of criticisms of the home civil service open to a Fulton Committee denied the opportunity to fully review the minister–civil servant relationship had a very familiar look too. One senior civil servant, Sir Edward Playfair, playfully rehearsed Fulton's findings a year before the report:

> The main function of the Civil Service today is management. The Administrative Class is something of a hangover from the past: splendid men of high intellect, but exclusively recruited from Oxbridge, subject to promotion from the Executive Class as a secondary source, and devoid of any management training, who find themselves in charge of great machines which they do not know how to control. They are too inbred. Scientists and professionals in the Civil Service are overlooked when it comes to promotion to top jobs: outsiders are practically never let in. There should be more interchange with the outside world; and the main cure for all these ills is to have a single managerial class which will run together today's Administrative and Executive Classes, with special provisions for late entry of graduates and others. There should be more elaborate provision for management training. [1]

The broad lines of any likely future reconstruction of the home civil service had been evident for some time before Fulton. The relative position of the administrative class had changed considerably since the heyday of Fisher, Dale and Laski. Important specialist groups, most notably the scientific officer class and the works group of professional classes, had been formed and had well-developed hierarchies, the leading posts in which, as often as not, required their holders to be 'chairborne' much like any other administrator. The higher civil service of 1939 had been more or less the same thing as the administrative class grades from assistant secretary upwards. Lawyers made up most of the remaining fringe. The administrative class still dominated the topmost posts of the service in 1955, but filled only about one-third of the posts of assistant secretary or better. The Priestley Commission, reporting in 1955, recommended treating the higher civil service as one for pay purposes. It seemed only a matter of time before the formal structure of the home civil service was changed in that direction. In addition, the administrative class was being undermined from below in two ways. First, it was failing to recruit sufficient numbers of direct entrants to replenish its ranks. Secondly, and largely as a consequence, it had much more recourse than previously to promotion from the executive class. By the time of Priestley, promotees numbered no less than 36 per cent of principals in the administrative class. In 1966 only 46 per cent of the administrative class had entered its ranks by the route of open competition to assistant principal, whereas 38 per cent had been promoted from below. In 1947 the executive and clerical hierarchies had been merged, with the natural promotion outlet of the clerical officer becoming the executive officer grade. The merging of the executive and administrative hierarchies seemed the logical next step, and one which was bound to encourage mergers elsewhere in the structure in the dissimilar cases of the scientific civil service and the works group and supporting classes. Indeed, such mergers were one feature of Fulton's structural proposals which aimed to secure the more flexible deployment of staff by replacing 'the present multitude of classes and their separate career structures by the creation of a classless, uniformly graded structure of the type that is now being adopted in many large business firms and similar to the system used by the Civil Service in the United States'. Fultón thought that 'some twenty grades could contain all the jobs from top to bottom in the non-industrial part of the Service'. This was 'essentially a pay structure' and 'not designed to determine the actual organization of work' which, as 'there should be no set pattern', was to be decided by job evaluation. Fulton wanted a system in which 'it should be possible to reward merit by extra pay as well as by promotion'. Within its proposed overall structure, and distinguishing as separate a senior policy and management group comprising the grades of under secretary and above, Fulton envisaged a range of occupational groups in place of the class system.[2]

While the Labour government of 1968 seemed disconcerted by the Fulton Committee's divisions over 'preference for relevance' in the related matter of direct-entry recruitment, it endorsed the committee's agreed recommendation in favour of a unified grading structure, as it did that for establishing a Civil Service College as a centre for, and as part of, an expansion of provision for post-entry training. The task of 'the reform of the Civil Service, taking full account of, but not bound by, what the Fulton Report had to say' was given to a committee of the service's National Whitley Council chaired by Sir William Armstrong. Like the Council's Reorganization Committee of 1920–1 (which had laid down the general outlines of the main part of the previous structure) the Armstrong Committee of 1968–73 was composed of senior civil servants and union representatives. Similarly, too, the

Armstrong Committee picked over the findings of an external inquiry and selected out what it deemed practicable. The setting up of the Civil Service College went ahead as planned and some changes were made in methods of recruitment. The sticking point came over the unified grading structure. The various mergers went ahead. The administrative, executive and clerical classes were merged to form the administration group on 1 January 1971. The scientific civil service was unified in the autumn of 1971 and the works group and associated classes were merged from the beginning of 1972. However, the examination of North American arrangements and those of some commercial organizations nearer home did not lead to the Armstrong Committee endorsing the introduction of a unified grading structure, except at under secretary level and above.[3]

The outcry from understandably frustrated Fultonites tended to obscure two things. One was that Fulton's assault on generalism and its preference for specialization seemed to point more to a break-up of the home civil service than to its unification primarily on the basis of pay. The other, with which I deal below, was the extent to which the structure and the recruitment and training arrangements of the civil service have changed in the past twenty years.

2   The Evolving Structure of the Non-Industrial Civil Service

Such has been the pace of change in recent years in the structure of the main part of the home civil service that, as we shall see, important developments have taken place, or are in definite prospect, since the beginning of 1982, the latest date at which, currently, it is possible to analyse that structure on the basis of detailed official statistics. These show that the non-industrial civil service numbered 532,805 then, being divided into the home civil service, which comprised 526,146 civil servants,[4] and the diplomatic service. While the structure of the diplomatic service remains much the same as that given to it by the Plowden Committee, the scale of the Armstrong changes in the 1970s has meant that in formal appearance the structure of the home civil service is now very different from that which Fulton reviewed, and in important respects resembled that which Fulton proposed.

This is certainly true of the 'open structure' established in 1972 at the very highest levels of the home civil service – meaning under secretary level and above – which seems the same as the senior policy and management group that Fulton recommended. The Armstrong

Committee's ambition was to create an 'open society' at the most senior levels of the service. Classes were abolished there and a system of unified grading introduced. In 1982 the 'open structure' numbered 736: 40 permanent secretaries (all men) including second permanent secretaries, 143 deputy secretaries (including 4 women), and 553 under secretaries (including 28 women). All job holders in the same grade are paid the same with small exceptions. Three permanent secretaries – the secretary to the Cabinet, the permanent secretary to the Treasury and the head of the home civil service – are paid more than the others. There are two intermediate pay points used where, for example, a post which would normally be graded under secretary has line control of another under secretary post. Appointments to deputy secretary and above are a shared responsibility between departments and the Management and Personnel Office (MPO). They are made with the approval of the Prime Minister, on the recommendation of the head of the home civil service, advised by senior colleagues on the Senior Appointments Selection Committee, after consultation and agreement with the departmental minister concerned, and with his permanent secretary where appropriate. Promotion to under secretary level is made by a permanent secretary of a department after consultation with the MPO and with the approval of the departmental minister concerned. There are no formal age or seniority constraints. Although talk of succession planning is in fashion, staff cuts have eroded career prospects at 'open structure' level. In recent years the percentage of personnel in the 'open structure' who are *not* former members of the administrative class or of the administration group has been stable at around 40 per cent. In 1981, for instance, aside from 4 per cent who had not been members of major groups, 3 per cent had formerly been in the economist group, 2 per cent in the statistician group, 6 per cent in the professional and technology group and related grades, 4 per cent in the medical group, 10 per cent in the science group, and 11 per cent in the legal group. These specialists normally remain within professional chains of command.[5]

The 60 per cent of 'open structure' posts held by civil servants with an administrative background were reviewed by the Wardale inquiry of 1981, instituted by the Thatcher government primarily it seems to establish whether or not the under secretary grade was really necessary. The Wardale inquiry recommended that 'no Open Structure grade should be abolished'. Compared with other organizations similar in size to a government department, where the 'open structure' had only three main grades, Wardale found that 6–10 would be the norm elsewhere. Wardale indicated the differences between the 'open structure' grades.

Permanent Secretaries focus in one place ultimate accountability for the work of all a department's officials, set with Ministers its tone and style, manage its resources, ensure that it is continuously able to do its job; provide, in the most important and sensitive areas, the last word of official advice to Ministers, ensure that they are served properly, ensure continuity as Ministers change, and represent the department in Whitehall and externally.

The second permanent secretary is a substitute for, not in line to, the permanent secretary. In the case of the Ministry of Defence he acts for the permanent under secretary because of pressure of work on that official, and in the case of the DHSS as head of department for the social security side. Wardale experienced 'considerable difficulty in ascertaining and accurately delineating the proper functions of the Deputy Secretary grade', because of 'the lack of clear definition of purpose of some posts and the multiplicity of roles undertaken by the grade'. The inquiry found that 'in some departments there were more deputy secretary posts than could readily be justified on the basis of the work . . . and this tended to obscure the real jobs to be done at this level'. These 'real jobs' occurred, first, where a major and closely interrelated area of work, possibly extending to several under secretary commands, needed a single focus below head of department level, an example being the Home Office Police Department. Secondly, the deputy secretary grade was justified where the need was 'to integrate substantial blocks of work which would otherwise have to be integrated by the head of department. Where integration is not possible the function of the second management level is to dispose, itself, of all but the most important business . . . so as to reduce to manageable proportions the amount falling to the head of department. The issue is the volume of work, not simply the numbers reporting. An example is Deputy Secretary (Administration) in DHSS.' Some posts not fulfilling these organizational roles as a management level also properly fall into the deputy secretary grade on job-weight grounds. Wardale said that 'Deputy Secretaries may become involved in what can be called the corporate or collegiate management of a department. They act almost as emanations of the Permanent Secretary, discussing with him and with Ministers a common approach to problems', and commanding 'sufficient authority both with Ministers and outside interests to act on behalf of the Permanent Secretary'. This role was likely to fall to deputy secretaries as individuals more than as holders of particular posts. Wardale found that 'Under Secretaries have very varied jobs. Strong jobs are closely identified with a coherent and discrete area with which the government has to be concerned continuously . . . They did the sort of job where the holder could be thought of as, say, "Mr Coal" and brought together a number of sub-elements relating to such an entity. Other Under Secretary jobs, less instantly recognizable were nonetheless similarly necessary.' For Wardale believed that

> the Under Secretary grade appears after searching scrutiny to be a vital one in many areas. There was a clear need for management and integration of work between Assistant Secretary and Permanent Secretary levels. There is an absolute need to ensure that policies are developed and co-ordinated in a systematic way, that compatible priorities are set for large areas of work and that Ministers receive coherent advice taking account of what is often a wide range of factors. This is what many Under Secretaries are doing and the work clearly has to be done . . . The work of government departments is extensive and complex. That work, whether of a policy or an operational nature, has to be managed, the important issues identified, and decisions obtained from Ministers or the heads of departments. It would be impossible to do without one management level, at least, in almost all areas. That level is, usually, provided by the Under Secretary grade; to provide it at Deputy Secretary level would undoubtedly dilute that grade.

Nevertheless, Wardale's overall conclusion was still that 'a number of Open Structure posts can be removed and should be'. Such a finding from an authoritative review would seem likely to encourage further cuts in the numbers from the 813 of 1980 to below the 736 of 1982 possibly to below the 718 of 1972 when that structure was established in its present form.[6]

That the old administrative class can be easily discerned within the existing form of the 'open structure', as well as lower down the service, too, has encouraged the belief that the structure of the home civil service has scarcely been changed at all. This is exaggerated. That service is less changed than it might have been had Fulton stuck to its reforming guns and consistently resisted the Treasury's scheme for the crucial administrative–executive–clerical merger and advanced its own scheme, arguing for it on the basis of the needs of the work to be done. Nevertheless, the government's announcement in 1983 that it wished to extend unified grading down to senior principal and its equivalents suggested that more of Fulton's ambitions may yet be realized. As it is, what seems to be widely unappreciated is not only the extent to which the structure of the home civil service below under secretary level has changed since Fulton's day, but also how much it has changed along lines which Fulton favoured. Of course, the basic unit in the structure still remains the grade and at every stage in his or her career a civil servant belongs to a particular grade. Grades remain grouped in larger structures according to the type of work involved. What is different about the main part of the structure of the home civil service compared with before 1971 is that whereas the former system was based on classes, the present structure is a mixture of classes of the older kind and the Armstrong system based on categories and occupational groups. As before 1971 a class is defined as a single grade, or a collection of grades linked in a recognizable hierarchy for career and management purposes, and for which separate recruitment arrangements are needed. There are three types of class: general services classes (the members of which are employed throughout the service or in a substantial number of departments); departmental classes (confined to a single department); and a few linked departmental classes (whose members are employed in more than one department although they are normally recruited and managed on a departmental basis). Almost half of these staff are accounted for by large departmental classes in the prison service and in the Inland Revenue tax inspectorate and other revenue branches. This class structure now exists alongside, and over 75 per cent of the non-industrial home civil service has been displaced by, the Armstrong system of occupational groups and categories. The administration group with 235,197 (134,515 females) accounted for 44·7 per cent of the home civil service in 1982 and dominated the general category – the remaining members of which drawn from the economist group, the information officer group, the librarian group and the statistician group, only numbering 2,398 altogether. The social security category/group is also large, comprising 48,320 (32,727 women) DHSS local office staff who receive a pay differential compared with their executive officer and clerical officer counterparts in the administration group from which the social security group was separated off in 1975. Large also is the secretarial category/group numbering 26,736 (all but 143 female). The professional and technology group was the largest of the specialist groups with 37,059 (240 women); the science category/group employing 15,273 (2,063 women), and the legal category numbering 716 (134 women). Of the specialist groups that most interested Fulton, the professional accountant class (381, including 6 women) was the last to be brought within the Armstrong structure.[7]

So, even though the unified grading structure has as yet only been introduced on a limited basis, it cannot be said that nothing has changed in the structure of the home civil service nor, given the similarities with the Armstrong structure, that it has not changed in line with some of Fulton's ideas. What does need to be stressed is that Fulton gave an important part of the structural game away at the outset and without a sufficiently serious contest. In Appendix F of its report, the Fulton Committee set out the case against 'starring' certain graduate entrants to the administrative side of the service, but conceded extra salary inducements for those so selected. This was lame enough, given Fulton's 'classless' aims, because the 'starred' entrants would be assistant principals in all but name. Worse followed, for in the text of its report, the committee said 'we propose the merger of the Administrative, Executive and Clerical Classes, as recommended to us by the Treasury'. Naturally enough, the reservations in Appendix F tended to be forgotten and this mattered because the Treasury proposals of 1966 looked very much like the structure which the Plowden Committee had recommended for the diplomatic service two years before. However, whereas Plowden was clear that the distinction between the various classes would persist, the Treasury maintained that they would disappear with the rationalization of the career ladders. Effectively, Fulton accepted this and the Armstrong changes included, as we have seen, the merger which established the administration group. Even the sceptical C. H. Sisson, lionizer of the generalist, seemed to be misled. For he complained at the time of the 1971 changes that 'the comedy of pseudo-egalitarianism goes so far that in order to do away with the shocking associations of the word Administrative the new style graduate entrants are to be called – illiterately – Administration Trainees'. While sensing that the changes would make little difference, Sisson, none the less, seemed to fear for these entrants' futures. Wigan seemed as likely a destination for them as Whitehall.[8]

A glance at the structure of the diplomatic service bequeathed by Plowden would have consoled him. The mainstream grades as at 1 January 1982 were as follows:

DS1	= permanent secretary	senior grades	150
DS2	= deputy secretary		
DS3	= under secretary		
DS4	= assistant secretary		287
DS5	= principal		453
DS6	= senior executive officer		281
DS7A	= higher executive officer (D)		625
DS7E	= higher executive officer		
DS8	= administration trainee		
DS9	= executive officer		815
DS10	= clerical officer		555

Source: Foreign and Commonwealth Office.

The administrative entrant to DS8 proceeds to DS7A and then, skipping DS6, to DS5 and up the ladder. The executive entrant to DS9 proceeds to DS7E and then to DS6. The clerical entrant follows him, one rung behind to start with. As Plowden said, having designed it: 'this scheme maintains separate Administrative, Executive and Clerical entry points and promotion streams. But it brackets grades in such a way as to make it difficult for anyone to be publicly labelled as in one stream or another'.[9]

The radically inclined on the Fulton Committee should not have effectively given their stamp of approval to the Treasury's proposals. They should have stamped on them. For those proposals perpetuated the administrative class in disguise. The formal abolition of the assistant principal grade was not the same as the abolition of the administrative class ladder. In all but name – and even that is not true of most of the grades – the old arrangements on the administrative side of the service as a whole have largely survived the introduction of the administration group. This is clear from the structure of that Group as at 1 January 1982 (numbers of women in brackets):

assistant secretary	1,052	(63)
senior principal	658	(14)
principal	4,035	(373)
senior executive officer	7,446	(564)
higher executive officer (D)	362	(105)
higher executive officer	22,021	(3,881)
administration trainee	274	(86)
executive officer	44,869	(17,458)
clerical officer	87,191	(58,896)
clerical assistant	67,469	(53,075)

Source: Civil Service Statistics 1982, p. 21.

The structure can best be understood from the perspective of the service's lower reaches. The natural promotion outlet from the clerical assistant grade remains the clerical officer grade, and from that grade the outlet remains the executive officer grade, alongside the minority recruited to that grade. For all executive officers – aside from a handful selected for higher things – the next steps in the ladder are the same as before: the grades of higher executive officer and of senior executive officer. The remainder of the well-developed executive hierarchy persists, too, even though the old grade names treasured by students of bureaucratic insignia have gone. The chief executive officer grade has been merged into that of principal. The senior chief executive officer grade has been renamed that of senior principal, and the principal executive officer grade has been merged with that of assistant secretary. Beyond this and, therefore, very near the top of the service there remains 74 staff in what are called executive directing grades and which are placed outside the administration group. So, the executive ladder, minus some impressive titles, continues to be there to be climbed by promotees from clerical officer, direct entrants to executive officer, and by those not marked out for fast promotion under the administration trainee scheme as it operated between 1971 and 1981. These 'unstarred' ATs then had the prospect of eventual arrival at principal level held out to them. The risk they ran of ending up in Wigan was fairly slender. The 'starred' entrants faced no risk at all. For they were assistant principals in all but name. This was made even more explicit from January 1982 with the introduction of the Administration Trainee and Higher Executive Officer (Development) Scheme, broadly along lines which an internal review committee had pressed for in 1978. Under the scheme, external recruitment to administration trainee was confined to a fast-stream entry of graduates under 28 with at least second-class honours degrees. The competition was also open within the same age limit to in-service candidates with similar degrees and non-graduates nominated by departments. There was also provision for selection from departmental nominees straight into the higher executive officer (D) grade. Entrants to the administration trainee grade remain there for two years, and those who complete this period of probation or trial service successfully are promoted to higher executive officer (D), and after a further two to three years they normally reach principal and, like the assistant principals of old, they can expect to reach at least assistant secretary rank eventually. [10]

The overriding reason why the administrative side of the home civil service needed to be reconstructed was because the pre-1971 arrangements took no account of the expansion of university education over the previous quarter of a century, an expansion which pre-dated Robbins. The service had been recruiting 'high fliers' at administrative level and taking in direct entrants with university entrance qualifications at executive officer level. There were very few openings in between. Moreover, while the service was turning away able graduates at the door, what could have been their places were taken by promotees from below, largely from an executive class which was itself dominated by promotees from below (and still is, to the extent of 74 per cent of entrants to the executive officer grade in 1981). This might not matter if the lower reaches of the service still attracted the numbers of talented people that they had done as late as the 1930s. There may still be low-ranking civil servants of the kind that Laski used to reminisce about, with the ability to secure first-class degrees in the evenings:[11] but, probably, proportionately, many fewer of them compared with his day. The expansion of the service and of outside opportunities, not least for more conventional university study, has undermined this source of talent. Ordinary graduate recruitment at executive officer level has increased dramatically in recent years. The pre-Armstrong structure, as it had developed since the War, had its advantages for the run-of-the-mill civil servant. Clerical assistants, clerical officers and executive officers could expect to reach executive officer, higher executive officer and senior executive officer respectively over a full career. They could do better with luck, ability, if the age structure was particularly favourable, or if government expanded at the right time, and worse if these factors were not operating. The prospects were hardly exciting, but it was all fairly safe. The class barriers protected the talentless. They acted like tariff walls against competition. For some class-to-class promotions the service had even run what were literally called 'limited competitions'. The Treasury proposals, and the creation of an administration group, were designed to let more graduates in. Instead of a few openings like the tax inspectorate, under the original administration trainee scheme the graduate not destined for the highest things had the prospect of a relatively swift advance of what was, except in name, the old executive ladder. This was not the stuff of revolution – but it did mean that in a central area of the service the Armstrong changes were substantial ones. A revolutionary change would have been to make all graduates start at executive officer with their progress dependent on their performance at work and in training rather than at the recruitment stage. It has to be remembered that Fulton did not advocate that, and insufficiently emphasized its reservations about the Treasury scheme which essentially was the same as the Armstrong structure.

The mergers which led to the creation of the science group (from the scientific officer, experimental officer and scientific assistant classes) and the professional and technology group (from the works group, the technical works, engineering and allied classes and the architectural and engineering draughtsman classes) were differently derived from that involving the administration group. In these cases, Fulton overrode Treasury evidence: but, in doing so, it was acting in accord with contemporary sentiment in favour of such mergers which largely seemed based on a desire for equity of treatment for specialists in relation to administrators. The relative deprivation of opportunities for specialists was a familiar theme in the standard reform case for the civil service which we saw Sir Edward Playfair identifying earlier. However, criticism of the kind that, for example, Fulton made about the limited role given to professional accountants in the service could not be simply dismissed as following fashion. As far as mergers involving the big classes of scientists and professionals were concerned, the Treasury was poorly placed to oppose them, having seemed to concede the merger case on the administrative side. Nevertheless, specialists were supposed to be recruited to the service to do work which their specialized knowledge fitted them for and not just to pursue careers. The real barrier between all but the exceptional scientific assistant or experimental officer and a principal scientific officer was not a class division but a gulf of knowledge, for which experience would be much less likely to compensate even than it would in administrative work. The formal equality of opportunity encouraged by the Armstrong structure has encouraged equality of expectation, the Holdgate Committee on the scientific civil service unsurprisingly found in 1980. Grades like senior scientific assistant and senior experimental officer, highly respected when the classes were separate are now it seems often seen as failure grades as the staff look beyond them up the ladder. Far from being allayed, as Fulton and others must have hoped, discontent about career opportunities in the scientific civil service is rife. The Holdgate Committee was aware of the difficulties of the merged structure, recognizing that 'the work of a senior laboratory technician . . . is not easy to compare with the work of a creative theoretician pushing forward the limits of knowledge – or with the work of a scientist in a central advisory team in an HQ organization'. With the wide range of work in the scientific civil service, whatever the structure, promotions would be bound to involve some comparison of unlikes. While the Armstrong structure maximized the potential for discontent, the Holdgate Committee proved unwilling to turn the clock back before Fulton.[12]

The scientific civil service is remarkable for its diversity of functions reflecting the fact that the government does not have a single science policy but a whole range of policies relating to, for example, defence, industry and agriculture. Government scientists do not form a homogeneous group or work in a uniform environment. Most of those undertaking and administering research and development, providing scientific services, or giving technical support to both, work in research establishments outside London. Most of those engaged in providing a technical contribution to policy or in determining and managing departmental research programmes work under chief scientists and controllers of research and development in departmental headquarters in London, Edinburgh, or Cardiff. The procurement executive of the Ministry of Defence is distinctive because it employs scientists in a continuum of activities (the equipment procurement process stretches from research through development and design to production, quality assurance and in-service support) in an integrated environment, embracing both research establishments and headquarters, that is available in no other department. Some 59 per cent of the scientific civil service is employed in the Ministry of Defence (which spends over half the total research and development funds of government), and that ministry's needs for scientists cover such a broad spectrum that it can provide a very wide range of career opportunities 'in house' compared with other government departments. The MOD also employs about 80 per cent of the civil service's professional engineers, who are to be found either side of the boundary between the science group and the professional and technology group, the majority in the latter. The MOD's procurement executive also employs over half of the professional accountants in the service.[13]

There have been several attempts in recent years to improve the relative position of specialists in the civil service. To act as a career focus, economists, accountants, statisticians, information officers and lawyers have a head of profession. Sir Alec Cairncross effectively acted in this role when he became head of the government economic service in 1964, and Fulton developed the idea later. While the lawyers as the longest established group of specialists in the service have always had a well-developed career hierarchy, the need to improve opportunities for the other groups has been pressed by the specialists themselves, their unions, reformers and various committees, including Fulton. The results have been unimpressive. To take a general example first, since 1972 'opportunity posts' have been designated in departments which are not considered to be limited to the work of one particular group or class but are open to suitably qualified and experienced staff in all groups or classes. Such posts give opportunities for specialists to gain a wider experience of management and administration. Yet, the experience of departments was of a decline in the numbers and quality of scientists applying for such posts. Holdgate wanted this trend reversed, but it could only suggest the creation of more posts. To take another example, under the Senior Professional Administrative Trainee Scheme (SPATS), also introduced in 1972, specialists who show the potential to reach the higher levels of the service are selected for special training and are given two years in an administrative or, occasionally, a managerial post. While the experience of other groups seems to have been more favourable, the 1970s witnessed a decline in the number of scientists training through the SPATS scheme. An official review observed in 1979:

> Scientists have traditionally been more reluctant than other specialists to work outside their specialism. With promotion opportunities less certain because of programme cuts in some areas, even fewer scientists have wanted to take the risk of a major career change and managers have been reluctant to encourage their good scientists to take it. Those who have taken the SPATS scheme have not always found that it met their expectations. Research evidence suggests that they have felt isolated from the scientific community, thought that they were regarded merely as short-stay administrators, and that their special skills were insufficiently valued, and in some cases have not found it easy subsequently to find scientific work which suited them.

The introduction of a special competition for specialists to achieve permanent transfer to the administration group was also unsuccessful in attracting scientists. On the other hand, as Holdgate observed, 'in recent years some 50 per cent or so of qualified scientists entering the Civil Service have elected to follow occupations that are not directly related to their degree specialism. Similarly, some 30 per cent of engineers have elected to work outside their professional discipline.' Holdgate believed that Lord Rothschild's view in 1972 that 'the great majority of qualified scientists who enter Government service do so because they want a scientific career" was no longer valid, although it might well apply to those entering the scientific civil service. 'It cannot therefore be true that scientific academic training necessarily restricts the subsequent career options of those who undertake it', Holdgate observed. 'Nor is it true that the Scientific Civil Service is the only source of supply for top management of those with a basic scientific training and approach.' If there had been a change, as the Holdgate evidence suggested, it had come in graduate recruitment at executive officer level. Such recruitment did not seriously offset the disappointments of initiatives like SPATS, or the fact that there is no definite sign of a lasting increase in the proportion of AT recruits with qualifications in science, mathematics, or engineering.[14]

The small number of professional accountants employed in the civil service and their lack of prominence was adversely commented on by Fulton. An inquiry by Sir Ronald Melville and Sir Anthony Burney, completed in 1973, showed that employment of the then professional accountant class was concentrated in the MOD and the Department of Trade and Industry, but also that the class included under half of the qualified accountants in the service. Most of the others were in the DoE's district audit service auditing local government expenditure. Internal audit in government departments outside the MOD has never been in the hands of professional auditors. To some extent, this is because the service has tended to develop its own specialized areas of accountancy. Hence, the training given to the tax inspectorate of the Inland Revenue and both internally and externally to the staff of the exchequer and audit department. In each case, as Melville–Burney found, the training programme and examination syllabus are tailored to the department's needs. However, the main explanation why, traditionally, the service has employed relatively few professional accountants lies in the role originally given to the former executive class. 'The Extended Use of the Executive Class' was a fitting title for the circular which gave details in 1947 of the merger of the executive and clerical classes. This was because the executive class was formerly only used restrictively on what the Reorganization Committee had called 'the higher work of supply and accounting departments, and of other executive or specialized branches of the service'. The executive class, including certain departmental executive classes such as that of the exchequer and audit department, had occupied most of the ground which professional accountants might have been expected to cover. In an attempt to secure more explicit professionalism (or, some thought, to make less visible the number of accountants employed), in July 1982 an accountancy functional specialism was established within the administration group staffed by an expanded government accountancy service comprising members of that group and all members of the former professional accountant class. [15]

Similar criticisms of the structure of the home civil service to those listed by Sir Edward Playfair before Fulton reported could be made now. That this is so is more than a matter of civil service obstruction of Fulton. As we have seen, on the perpetuation of the administrative class in disguise Fulton helped to dig the grave for its own ambitions. The structure of the home civil service is bound to be complex, having to include not just administrators, managers and clerks, but many different kinds of them. It also includes not just specialists, but many different kinds of specialist, so that a body such as the science group is markedly heterogeneous in composition in terms of discipline. There are also a host of groups such as prison governors and prison officers and HM inspectors of schools which are not readily merged with others.

While some of the pre-Armstrong demarcations may have been obstructive, the decisive factor behind any changes ought not to be pay and careers on the Fulton model, but the work – the complex range of duties of civil servants. For instance, important though it remains to give as many opportunities as possible for administrative talent in the specialist group to be utilized, the work must come first; and only limited results can be expected from developments such as the establishment of integrated hierarchies whether in the pre-Fulton Ministry of Transport or in the DOE afterwards. Interchange between specialists and generalists can only really be one way and needs justification. The MOD pointed out to the Finniston Committee on the engineering profession in 1978 that British private companies made relatively little use of engineers at senior management levels. If Fulton wanted the civil service to act as an example in overriding what seems to be a cultural prejudice it should have argued for that. Changing the educational system so that science and engineering does attract more talent would seem not only a more direct but also a more appropriate policy. The civil service employs some 5 per cent of the nation's scientists and some 3 per cent of her engineers; but there is no evidence that it attracts more than its fair share of the cream.[16] Even if traditional prejudices favouring the generalist were weaker than they are, it would be surprising if the conventional type of administrator recruited by a severe competition did not prevail in appointments to the leading posts in the service against specialists not so recruited; and it is to the recruitment system that we now turn.

3   The Pattern and Problems of Direct-Entry Recruitment to the Civil Service

'The dominance of Oxford and Cambridge graduates still continues in the Administrative Class', W. A. Robson complained at the time of the centenary of the Trevelyan–Northcote Report, 'Is this possibly due to most of the examiners being appointed from those universities?' Professor Robson's remarks reflect the controversy that direct-entry recruitment to the upper reaches of the civil service tends to attract. Fulsome praise of the open competitive principle often seems to be followed by severe criticism of its practice. Few fail to approve of the fact that the Civil Service Commission was established in 1855 to provide the central machinery through which, especially after 1870, nepotism was gradually replaced by open competition as the predominant method of recruitment to the service. Despite the extent to which the service came to relate its structure and recruitment arrangements to the various stages of the educational system, it has never been solely composed of open competition entrants directly selected by the commission from that system's products. It was not so composed as late as 1914, and then came the disruption of war and after it of special competitions to admit ex-armed forces entrants; a pattern that was repeated within the Second World War. Now, even if one disregards the small number of politically and hence temporarily appointed special advisers, the civil service will never be entirely composed of centrally recruited open competition entrants. Ninety per cent of recruitment is done by the employing departments. The 10 per cent of recruitment left to the Civil Service Commission tends to be for the higher posts, prominently, of course, including those in the diplomatic service and in what was the administrative class area that are commonly regarded by critics as preserves of the upper-middle-class, privately educated arts graduates of Oxbridge.[17]

The Civil Service Commission is now located within the Management and Personnel Office, having not been a separate body since 1968 when it was made part of the CSD. At that time, the House of Commons was assured by the then Prime Minister that 'in matters of recruitment policy the First Commissioner is responsible to Ministers in the normal way. He and his staff are working closely together with those in the Department responsible for personnel management and training. In matters of selection – that is, when acting as Commissioners considering individual cases – they will continue to have exactly the same independence as they have had before.' If things were really to be much the same, why make the change? One reason was that without the commission the CSD would have been even thinner on functions. Another reason may have been to try to inject more life into the commission, whose representatives had seemed bemused by their role when the Select Committee on Estimates had reviewed civil service recruitment in 1965. For the commission, for a time, things seemed hectic. As its official historian almost breathlessly remarked: 'Absorbed into CSD, restructured on a line management basis and moved to Basingstoke all within the space of two years, this probably provided the most radical upheaval that the Commission had experienced since 1855.' For most of its previous history the commission had been able to act like a privileged schoolmaster who, at a leisurely pace, and through his own examination papers, could select the cream from the wealth of talented young people only too keen to enter a prized occupation. Full employment changed that. The commission's examining role was gradually relinquished. A clerical class competition without written examination was introduced for London posts as early as 1953, became continuous in 1955 and then countrywide in 1956. The last academic examination for the clerical class was held in 1966. The age limits for clerical recruitment eventually came to range from 16 to 59. Now, departments have the option of recruiting clerical assistants and clerical officers on the basis of academic qualifications (2 acceptable GCE O level passes and their equivalents, and 5 similar passes respectively), followed by an interview; or by means of a short answer test followed by a similar interview. The last academic examination for the executive class was held in 1963, and for the administrative class (the old Method I) in 1969. The sole means of entry to the AT grade for young people from outside the service then became the former Method II competition, which the commission had first introduced in 1948, basing it on wartime army officer selection procedures. Method II was 'a selection system to which the Public Service can point with pride', the Davies Committee said in 1969, thus praising the commission for its boldest initiative in the postwar period, and one made in the area of administrative recruitment most subject to outside criticism. The commission's difficulties, in fact, were greater in the area of recruiting specialists. In the commission's annual reports in its last years as a separate entity, its historian-remarked, 'references to the shortfall in the recruitment of quantity surveyors, engineers, accountants, lawyers, architects, and statisticians appear with monotonous frequency'. Moreover, 'the failure to fill posts was not the only disturbing factor. There was a failure to attract a sufficient proportion of entrants to the specialist classes who in the opinion of the selection boards were of really high quality, and anxiety was expressed about who within the Service would prove capable of filling the senior professional posts in the future.' From 1971 onwards the service made more effort through graduate trainee schemes to produce its own specialists and, as in other areas, the end of full employment improved recruitment generally: but the legacy of the lean years remains. Similar shortfalls in recruitment seem likely to have resulted in comparable difficulties in the scientific civil service, although the Holdgate Committee emphasized that 'individual research establishments within the Service . . . are recognized national centres of excellence; they are thus extremely attractive to scientists and have little difficulty . . . in attracting good candidates'.[18]

Decentralized recruitment procedures now predominate in the civil service. They began in 1964 when clerical officer vacancies were filled for the first time by means of local competitions arranged and advertised by the departments concerned. After that, the Civil Service

Commission increasingly delegated recruitment responsibilities to the departments, subject only to checking on aspects of candidates' eligibility. Even this role was removed by the Civil Service Order in Council 1982 under which, from the beginning of 1983, departments now have the sole responsibility for recruitment, except for those grades which have a mobility obligation (meaning, a requirement for the staff concerned to be prepared to transfer from one part of the country to another). Thus, centralized recruitment by the Civil Service Commission is limited to levels broadly equivalent to executive officer and above, about 10 per cent of total recruitment. In 1982, for example, this still meant that the commission conducted 277 competitions, involving 119,434 applications and 5,352 appointments, and that it still has substantial responsibilities for the recruitment of graduates and of those with professional qualifications.[19]

The big explosion in graduate recruitment in recent years has been at executive officer level. The commission once described the EO entry as a barometer of the national employment climate, and as economic conditions in the 1970s worsened so the formal quality of the intake has improved. Candidates for EO must be between 17½ and 44 and as a minimum possess or secure university entrance qualifications, preference being given in the case of grade 9 of the diplomatic service to those with foreign-language qualifications. All candidates have to take qualifying tests before proceeding to an interview. Such has been the recent pressure of graduate interest that since 1980 the commission has introduced separate competitions to safeguard the school-leaver entry. Graduates and undergraduates accounted for 55 per cent of the EO entry in 1982. Moreover, the latest published research findings – for 1979 – showed that 83 per cent of the graduate entry had obtained honours degrees (22 per cent had either firsts or good seconds). There were more arts graduates selected than others, although there were more science graduates declared successful than those in English or history. Not surprisingly, the EO graduate entry was more representative of the higher education system than that for AT. While the success ratio of Oxbridge candidates was impressive, all the UK universities provided some entrants. London provided five times the Cambridge total, and Portsmouth Polytechnic had only 2 successes fewer than Oxford, which was well down the list. The diplomatic service has always looked to its executive stream for its middle managers and, now that the AT entry has been reduced to the fast stream only, the home civil service will increasingly have to revert to doing the same. That service's overall graduate intake even into its administration group is not Oxbridge dominated. Of the 33 graduates among the 40 in-service appointees to the AT grade in 1979, for instance, 8 were London graduates and Oxford and Cambridge supplied only 2 and 3 respectively. While the number of such appointees fell to a total of 3 (one Oxbridge) in 1982 under the changed AT arrangements, 1,000 graduates still came in at EO level.[20]

Naturally, though, outside interest and criticism concentrates on the social, school and university origins of, and the studies previously pursued by, those external entrants to the home civil service designed as high fliers either as members of a wider AT graduate entry as between 1971 and 1981, or as members of the fast-stream-only AT entry since them. Only the diplomatic service, the high fliers of which are recruited by similar methods, attracts anything like the attention which outside critics have lavished on the external graduate AT entry and its forerunner. Fulton gave its attention to little else, making several criticisms of the selection procedures, with a majority of the committee unsuccessfully urging the government to introduce 'preference for relevance' in recruitment to what was to be AT level. That area of recruitment has attracted no fewer than three committees of inquiry since Fulton. The first, in 1968–9, and already referred to, was led by J. G. W. Davies (a former secretary of the Cambridge University Appointments Board), which found 'no evidence of bias' in the then Method II. The second committee of inquiry, ten years later, was chaired by the then First Civil Service Commissioner, F. H. Allen, to deal specifically with the criticisms made by, and in evidence to, the English Committee. The third inquiry, led by Sir Alec Atkinson, a former senior civil servant in 1982–3, reviewed the changed recruiting arrangements at and around AT level, with an emphasis on making them more cost-effective. The numbers of AT entrants being sought have declined from 160 in 1978 to 44 in 1982, which is roughly how many assistant principals used to be recruited in the 1950s. The most popular degree subjects represented amongst successful candidates in 1982 were history, economics (including PPE) and English. No classics graduate was successful. The days of the Greats man dominating the entry has gone. However, the predominance of Oxbridge (and especially Oxford) continued: 16 out of the 21 successful external AT entrants were educated there.[21]

Three biases existed in recruitment to AT, the English Committee was told by Lord Crowther-Hunt: namely, preferences in favour of Oxbridge graduates, former pupils of fee-paying schools, and arts rather than social or natural science graduates. The Allen Committee was, essentially, set up to defend the commission's selection procedures against these stock criticisms and, as long as it was a general entry to AT that was being discussed, it was in little danger of losing the argument. It argued from the 1978 recruitment figures which, incidentally, showed that Oxbridge provided 52 per cent of the successful AT candidates.[22]

The first of the three stages of the AT competition is the qualifying test (QT) which lasts for a day and a half. It is the stage at which most of the variation in the success rates of candidates from different educational backgrounds occurs: for example, 50 per cent of Oxbridge candidates passed the QT in 1978 compared with 22 per cent of candidates from other universities. The QT consists of five objectively marked intelligence tests (the marking being a mechanical operation, requiring the examiner to exercise no judgement because answers are simply right or wrong), and three written papers. The Allen Committee pointed up the difficulties of those trying to argue that the QT was a source of unjustifiable bias against certain categories of candidate:

> In the first place, objectively-marked intelligence tests account for 45 per cent of the total marks. It is possible (and in practice not uncommon) for candidates to reach the aggregate pass mark by dint mainly of a good performance in these tests. As for written papers, anonymous marking eliminates the possibility of unfair discrimination − conscious or unconscious − on the part of the examiners (most of whom are non-Oxbridge university academics). By definition, of course, the written papers require the candidate to express himself on paper and this might be held to give an advantage to those well schooled in essay writing. However, in only one of the three papers − the Summary − are drafting skills important and even then they are considerably less important than precise analytical thought, the capacity for which is highly valued by departments. Moreover, the second written test (in terms of the marks it carries) is a test of the candidate's ability to draw valid inferences from statistical information. The candidates most likely to have the advantage here are the scientists and, to some extent, the social scientists. In practice, the written papers taken together account for less of the variation in success-rates between Oxbridge graduates and others than do the intelligence tests.

The Allen Committee's conclusion, unsurprisingly, was that 'the present QT is fair, and manifestly so'.[23]

The candidates who obtain the required aggregate mark in the QT are then invited to attend the second stage, a series of tests and interviews at the Civil Service Selection Board (CSSB) lasting for two days. Here, the candidates are divided into groups, usually of five, each group being examined by a team of three assessors who comprise a chairman, a psychologist and an observer. Over the two days the candidate takes further intelligence tests, does two written exercises, participates in two group exercises and has a forty-minute interview with each of the three assessors. The assessors then make an overall assessment of each candidate's suitability for appointment, taking account of all the available evidence, including school, university and personal references. The Allen Committee said that 'only one of the CSSB tests gave us cause for concern as a possible source of unfair discrimination between candidates from different educational backgrounds. This is the test of general information.' Even then, it was satisfied that 'in practice, interpretation of performance in the test is careful and sensitive'. Others might think differently. However, the committee was able to point out that 'at CSSB the candidate takes four intelligence tests and his or her scores in these, together with his or her scores in four of the intelligence tests taken in the QT, are combined to form indices which objectively measure basic intellectual equipment and capacity to learn new skills and broaden knowledge. Half of these tests are non-verbal tests which are relatively little influenced by differences in education and social environment.' As for the written and oral exercises,

the major written exercise – the Appreciation – is primarily a rigorous test of the candidate's ability to assimilate and organize intelligently a mass of information related to a simulated problem of public administration. The major oral exercise – the Committee Exercise – also provides valuable evidence about candidates' ability to cope with such problems as well as about their effectiveness – or potential effectiveness – in working with other people. It is, of course, undeniable that some candidates may perform below their potential in these exercises for a variety of reasons including oral and written inarticulacy, diffidence and naivety about political, social and economic issues. But these weaknesses, precisely because they limit the candidate's ability to deal with Civil Service problems and working methods, must be taken into account. Follow-up work by the Commission has in fact shown that the CSSB assessment of job aptitude, based on performance in these exercises, is effective in predicting departments' assessment of ATs' performance – and potential – after they have been appointed. We were therefore satisfied that the CSSB exercises are fair.

The English Committee described the CSSB procedure as depending more on interviewing than on written examinations. In fact, 'interviews occupy only one-fifth of candidates' time at CSSB. Nor are interviews given disproportionate weight. Interview evidence is always evaluated in the light of all the other evidence available to the assessors.' The Allen Committee believed that 'the very thoroughness of this procedure represents the best guarantee of its impartiality'. The committee also met the argument that

> however fair the CSSB procedure is in itself, those who work within it may have a natural, and possibly largely unconscious, affinity with candidates from the same cultural and social background. On this basis, an explanation for the relatively high success rate of Oxbridge graduates would be sought in the university background of the CSSB assessors. But analysis of their backgrounds does not support such an explanation: some two-thirds of the 1978 observers and over half of the psychologists attended universities other than Oxford and Cambridge. Similar proportions of the 1978 observers and psychologists attended maintained as opposed to independent schools. It would therefore be rare for teams of assessors not to contain at least one assessor with a non-Oxbridge, maintained school background.[24]

All candidates deemed acceptable by the CSSB, and those falling just short of an acceptable standard, go on to the third and concluding stage which is a thirty-five-minute interview with the Final Selection Board (FSB). The FSB's main function is to review all the evidence on a candidate, in particular the reports from the CSSB assessors, and award the final mark. The FSB interview is used primarily as an occasion for exploring areas of doubt or of strength and weakness revealed in the earlier evidence and not for making an independent judgement of the candidate. The Allen Committee was swift to point out that 'at the FSB stage there is no difference between the success rates of candidates from different educational backgrounds. This, despite the form of the FSB stage, which, prima facie, offers the greatest scope for subjective assessment of all the three stages.' Members of the FSB are drawn from four panels: the academic panel, the general panel and two panels of senior civil servants – the line managers and those with responsibilities for personnel. The membership of these panels changes as frequently as is consonant with experience of FSB work. The academic panel is drawn from a broad range of universities and polytechnics. The general panel is drawn from people in a wide variety of occupations, with private industry and commerce and the trade unions well represented. Members of the professions have been less well represented. In the great majority of cases the CSSB mark is endorsed by the FSB. The record shows that the FSB changes slightly more than 20 per cent of the marks recommended by the CSSB; and about half of these changes do not influence a candidate's success or failure in the competition. Subsequent research shows that FSB marks bear closer relation to subsequent departmental assessments of ATs than CSSB marks do.[25]

While the Allen Committee's scarcely concealed delight in handing out a drubbing to the service's critics was understandable, its conclusions were modified in some respects by the findings of the Civil Service Commission's own recruitment research unit. These are worth quoting in full.

The AT selection process is successful in predicting performance at work in the sense that Annual Confidential Report (ACR) ratings prove to be statistically related to FSB marks, without being totally determined by them. Job quality is also an important contributor to the ACR rating. It seems true to say that another aspect of the efficacy of the selection process is that it successfully performs the dual task of selecting people who *can* do the job, and keeping out those who cannot. As with all high grade selection, however, there is a corollary to this. The nature of the statistical relationship is such that, although ineffective candidates are identified and rejected, it is a virtual certainty that a number of candidates who would in fact have made capable ATs will be rejected along with them. The relationship between performance in the qualifying stage and the eventual selection decision, whilst mathematically of the same order as that between selection-performance and ACR ratings, is somewhat different in its implications. Here, passing the QT is clearly no guarantee of effectiveness in the CSSB/FSB stage. At the same time, though, it is again the case that amongst those who fail will be a number who, had they proceeded to the next stage, would have been selected for the job. The difference is in the nature of the tests. The CSSB/FSB procedure aims at testing across a wide range of ability, aptitude and attitude; the QT is very much narrower in its focus. At CSSB and FSB account can be taken of such items as interpersonal relations, emotional stability, maturity, drive, determination, influence; in the QT, despite the skillful inferences drawn on some of these topics from an examination of the discursive scripts, the thrust of the enquiry is mainly intellectual. Only after successfully negotiating this first, intellectual, hurdle can the candidate be judged on the way he deploys all the other personal resources available to him. In a sense, this is the wrong way round. A first sieve would ideally take the form of a wide-ranging, though not necessarily highly accurate, examination of a number of broad issues — it would include both intellectual, interpersonal, and intrapersonal enquiry. The subsequent stage would use a finer focus, and might specialize more on different broad areas for different jobs. Clearly, though, there are practical problems, and the fact that it is easier to centre on the intellectual area for mass-test administration. Mass enquiry into the other two areas would also demand pencil-and-paper practices, and issues of predictive validity would become more difficult still. The issue may have to rest with the consoling thought that the present QT does have a degree of predictive power with respect to the eventual decisions.[26]

Of course, this consolation may not be so readily appreciated by those turned down, especially now that the wider graduate entry to AT has been abandoned, leaving the executive officer entry as the next step down.

What the evidence that the Allen Committee assembled did do was dispel what it called 'the myth that the higher entry to the Home Civil Service is prejudiced in favour of Oxbridge, the public schools and the arts graduate'. As it recorded: 'the dominant statistical bias noted was in favour of the Oxbridge candidate and the greatest disparity occurred at the QT stage. A small statistical bias was detected in favour of former pupils of fee paying schools.' Taking the QT first, there was no significant variation in the performance of arts, science and social science graduates. Candidates with firsts did better than those with seconds who did better than those with thirds. Oxbridge graduates did better than other graduates. Former pupils of direct grant schools did better than former pupils of maintained schools. Independent school pupils had an intermediate success rate, but the performance differentials between direct grant and independent school pupils and between independent and maintained school pupils were not statistically significant. At CSSB, neither degree subject nor university had a statistically significant effect on their own, but there was an effect when the two were taken in combination. The Oxbridge social science graduate did better than social scientists from other universities, while Oxbridge scientists were less successful than scientists from other universities. At CSSB, as in the QT, candidates with better degrees did better than those with less good degrees, while there was no significant variation in the performance of candidates from different types of school. At the FSB stage, there were no significant variations in the performance of candidates on the basis of degree subject, degree class, university, or school.[27]

There is inequality of prestige between universities, and Lord Crowther-Hunt, currently rector of Exeter College, Oxford, himself observed that 'if the Civil Service is seeking to recruit the most able people it is hardly surprising that Oxbridge supplies a higher proportion than other universities'. The Allen Committee put it gently:

> most academic institutions have a share of exceptionally talented students, but some attract higher proportions than others: and some educate and train their students in ways that make them better prepared for the administration of public business. Oxford and Cambridge Universities in particular attract a disproportionately large number of the ablest school leavers and it can be argued that their collegiate and tutorial system of education does much to develop not only the intellectual but also the personal qualities that are desirable in a sound administration.

There is also a strong tradition in those universities of sending candidates forward. Oxbridge accounted for 25 per cent of the candidates in 1978, although its proportion of the honours undergraduate population was only 11 per cent. What currently concerns the commission more than continued Oxbridge successes is that, as measured by FSB marks, the quality of recent intakes seems to have been declining. In contrast, the CPRS thought that the diplomatic service attracted a greater share of talent than its work required. Between 1974 and 1981 the diplomatic service took 71 per cent of its administrative intake from Oxbridge disproportionately from 'towards the top of the social tree'.[28]

'Despite the recession, competition to employ the best graduates has become even keener over the past few years', the Atkinson inquiry reported in 1983. The best argument against 'preference for relevance' in recruitment at the time that a Fulton Majority recommended it – as the CPRS later did for the diplomatic service – was not that all subjects are 'relevant', even ancient languages, as the Civil Service Commission's historian implied.[29] It was and is that the home civil service at least was having sufficient problems in attracting talent anyway without limiting the field, and that it was best to rely on post-entry training to remedy deficiencies in the entrants' knowledge and skills. It is to such training that I turn below, bearing in mind that once one broke away from a general entry, 'preference for relevance' would look rather different.

4 The Pattern and Problems of Post-Entry Training in the Civil Service

'We have nothing to compare with the *Ecole Nationale d'Administration* in Paris', W. A. Robson lamented about the provision for post-entry training in the British civil service in 1956, much as a successor could still do now. The classic British attitude towards public administration is that it is 'something only to be learned by doing' — Sisson's actual words in 1966. A director of training and education had been appointed in the Treasury in 1945, following the Assheton Committee's review of civil service training made in 1944. What, importantly, Assheton had declined to do was to lend its support to contemporary agitation for a Civil Service College. This helped to ensure that for nearly twenty years afterwards central training provision even for trainee administrators remained very minor in scale — modest enough, in fact, to attract Sisson's approval. Training at departmental level seemed modest in scale, too, while dominating such provision as there was. This departmental dominance has proved to be a persistent feature of post-entry training in the civil service. In 1981/2, for instance, departments provided 76 per cent of such training compared with 20 per cent bought externally and only 4 per cent accounted for by the Civil Service College. That college had grown out of the Treasury's Centre for Administrative Studies established in 1963, about which, Sisson had observed, what was, at first, brief tuition for young administrators 'unaccompanied by any change in the method of recruitment has certainly not changed the character of the Service nor was it meant to do so'.[30] The Civil Service College opened in 1970 — following a Fulton recommendation — was envisaged as acting as a catalyst promoting a changed civil service. In this role it was doomed to disappoint, for it was not the Anglicized version of the Ecole Nationale d'Administration (ENA) that such an ambition demanded.

As the ENA has become established as the yardstick by which to measure civil service training developments in Britain, it seems best to indicate at the outset what the ENA is, and what it does, and a little of its history. Down to 1945, 'learning by doing' was dominant in both

Britain and France. The French compensated for this because the entrance examinations separately organized by the Grands Corps – the Conseil d'Etat, the Inspection des Finances, the Cour des Comptes – and by the departments all required specialized knowledge from candidates. Yet, as the ENA's director of studies, André Bertrand, almost incredulously later recorded, 'it was in France, and not in Great Britain, that a civil servant's training school was set up in 1945'. It was hoped to emulate the comparatively greater degree of unity achieved in the British civil service and generalizing the entrance requirements to the extent that the *licence en droit* was not compulsory was seen as a step in the British direction, too. Knowledge of the law and the social sciences merely remained a massive advantage. Michel Debré, the creator of the ENA, seems to have looked towards Britain, but the model he followed was a French one – the Ecole Polytechnique. Far from realizing the democratizing ambitions of the time, such a model was bound to mean the usual French combination of social and intellectual élitism would prevail. The external entry to the higher civil service as before is dominated by the products of the Parisian upper middle class educated at the Institut d'Etudes Politiques (the old Sciences-Po in nationalized form). They normally go further and faster in their careers than the in-service entrants to the ENA, the introduction of a special entry for whom put an end to straight line promotions and, in practice, inhibited the social mobility which the reformers were looking for. Far from ending the compartmentalization of the upper reaches of the French civil service, the reformers of 1945 added the division between the Grands Corps and the corps of *administrateurs civils*, the prestige of, and career prospects available in, the former being much superior to the latter and, hence, they attract the cream of the ENA graduates.[31] So the ENA seems to have been a disappointment compared with the ambitions of the reformers, while providing an effective means of satisfying the ambitions of its most successful products. Its French critics seem to be numerous, but then so do its British admirers.

Fulton was an admirer: 'the achievement of the French Civil Service with the ENA . . . is to have broken away from the traditional mould and created a vocational education for a modern Civil Service.' The 1971 reforms have changed the ENA compared with when Fulton admired it. Since the autumn of 1972 there have been four parallel competitions for entry to the ENA: separate competitions for external graduate candidates with legal training and for those trained in economics and related subjects, and similar competitions for serving officials. Not less than one-third and not more than one-half of the

ENA places are reserved for the latter. The qualifying competition is entirely written and, whichever competitive route is taken, candidates are asked to display high levels of knowledge of economics and the social sciences in general as well as of at least one foreign language. For the survivors, these types of knowledge are essential if they are to successfully negotiate the various hurdles of the largely oral entrance examination tests, to which are added physical exercise tests. The various papers and tests are carefully weighted and the written examinations offer little or no choice of topic. The 130 to 150 survivors of this intellectual endurance test (plus up to 2 highly placed products of the Ecole Polytechnique) enter the ENA in January of Year One. After a brief introductory course, the students normally spend the rest of the year *en stage* working in a *préfecture* and then either in another type of administrative authority at home or in French embassy abroad, or in a local authority in Britain or Western Germany. The students return to the ENA in January of Year Two destined to study there for most of the time until their course finishes in May of Year Three. While several of their courses are common, the students are divided into two sections: general administration and economic administration. All are required to study the practice of administrative decision-making, both in its general, legal aspect and specifically in terms of budgetary and financial decisions; and to study, too, the practice of negotiation, both internationally and between the 'social partners' in France. All students also study some of the sociological and psychological aspects of organizations, prior to a ten-week attachment to a commercial organization or company – the *stage d'entreprise*. All students, too, have to study at least one modern foreign language in depth (two for those with diplomatic career ambitions). All students also have to participate every week in some form of active sport. In addition to this core curriculum, the students, according to their section, engage in specialized studies, receiving tuition in relevant subjects and undertaking seminar work. For general administration students the main field is modern methods of management, and includes an introduction to applied mathematics and statistics, business accounting and computers. The economic administration students have more extensive programmes in both accounting and computer science, as well as a programme of applied mathematics and statistics, and a course in national income accounting and macro-economic forecasting. In addition, the students have to take two optional subjects undertaken by detailed group study (students with diplomatic career ambitions must select subjects with international connections). The examinations on the options count for 20 per cent of the total assessment mark. The marks for the examinations on the common core and the section programmes count for 64 per cent. The first-year stage counts for 14 per cent and the *stage d'entreprise* for 2 per cent. On the basis of the results, the students are ranked in order of merit, the order largely determining the choice of careers open to them.[32]

It would be difficult to translate an institution like the ENA, so much part of French culture, to Britain: but should this be attempted, as Fulton implied that it should, while neglecting to show how, then a British ENA could take the following form. It would be, like the original, a recruitment *and* training agency, singling out the ablest from a wide graduate entry, together with others from within the service, on the basis of performance within training. Such training would begin immediately on entry for outsiders and should last for two and a half years. The first nine months would consist of a common course at the Civil Service College. About half of this course would consist of a detailed study of public administration. Trainees would learn in detail about the functions of all the government departments and about their divisions and branches and, where applicable, their regional and/or local office systems. This part of the course would include instruction in that part of parliamentary procedure which can be formally taught. All entrants should know how the House of Commons works. This part of the course would also include a detailed study of the functions of local authorities and the public corporations. Besides public administration, trainees would also have to obtain a sound grounding in economics, statistics and management techniques. There would then be an examination covering the whole area of study and the unsuccessful would be required to leave the service or, in the case of internal trainees, to revert to the routine career flow. The survivors would then move on to the second part of the course which would consist of one year of practical experience. The first six months would be spent working closely with a principal in the headquarters of a government department, devilling for him, and in a much more closely supervised manner than has been traditional. The second six months would be spent in either a regional or local office of a government department, or in a local authority, or in a nationalized industry, or in private industry or commerce, doing a specific job. At the end of the year, the supervisors would make reports about the trainees, and copies would be made available to them so that they could review their progress. Those who survived the examination and the report stages would be assigned to government departments on the basis of their performance at the college and their own preferences, and then proceed to the last stage of the training course. All trainees would receive a common course developing their knowledge of management techniques, statistics and economics. In the case of economics, they should be taught to the level at which they can discuss the British economy professionally. The remainder of the course would be divided into specialisms: for example, those intended for careers in departments relating to social services would study social policy and administration and social statistics. At the end of this second nine-month course, another examination would form part of the overall final assessment of the trainees who would then proceed to posts in those departments for the duties in which they had been trained.

Central training in the British civil service has never taken this form, and Fulton took no steps to ensure that anything so arduous or so specialized was required. Civil service training was no longer a desert when Fulton surveyed it. The establishment of the Centre for Administrative Studies (CAS) in 1963 had ended the era of aridity and it was a flourishing oasis from which fertile developments could be expected. From an initial twenty-three weeks of instruction, the CAS handed on to the Civil Service College a training programme for assistant principals involving forty-four weeks of tuition. This comprised a four-week introductory course taken in the first year of service, covering quantitative analysis and the structure of government; a twelve-week course, usually taken in about the third year of service, in topics under the general heading of government and organization; and a twenty-eight-week course, consisting of twenty-two-weeks study of economic and social administration followed by one of a range of six-week extension courses in more specialized areas of study, normally taken in the fourth or fifth year of service. The Treasury's Osmond Committee, reporting in 1967, had recommended more training provision and using the CAS as the basis for 'an organization which . . . will give the Civil Service a Staff College, which many have advocated'. Osmond felt that it could do 'no more than try to map the lines of advance' and left others to work out 'detailed plans'. What had been 'lightly sketched will need to be filled in'. Surveying the terrain properly was Fulton's job, but it never really added anything to Osmond's 'sketch'. If Fulton wanted something akin to the ENA to be established, it should have argued for it, not least because of the opposition of the civil service unions to anything resembling a Higher Civil Service College. The Civil Service College, established as Fulton recommended, ended up trying to be all things to everybody with little initial gratitude for its efforts. Hence, specialists accepted for the SPATS programme receive a twelve-week course in administration and executive and clerical officers can take a five-day course in statistical skills. As an inquiry by R. N. Heaton and Sir Leslie Williams pointed out in 1974, Fulton and then the Wilson and Heath governments had wanted the Civil Service College to be

> a large scale and broad-based institution. As such, it has been expected to provide a very widely assorted range of courses, more varied, probably, than those of any comparable institution in this country and of such a divergent nature as to generate not a little ambiguity, and even some inner contradictions in its role. All this for a very large and constantly changing body of trainees of very widely varying abilities, experience and degrees of commitment and enthusiasm. It is as though some institution were expected to combine the role of All Souls and an adult education centre, with some elements of technical education and teacher training thrown in for good measure.

The college eventually became more widely respected, at least within the civil service; the initial experience of making its principal an academic rather than a serving officer not being repeated.[33]

The post-entry training provision for ATs which, in 1971, was planned as two fifteen-week multidisciplinary blocks, has been whittled down in recent years and in September 1981 what had become the pattern of two block release eight-week courses was replaced by a modular scheme of fast-stream training. This now comprises twelve separate modules offering a total of twenty-two weeks of training. After about three months in their departments, ATs can take an induction course in administration, comprising three modules, preferably run consecutively and consisting of communication skills and the use of information (one week), Parliament, government and the civil service (two weeks) and finance and control of public expenditure (one week). From their second year of service onwards, the ATs can take, separately if so chosen, up to six foundation modules: essential quantitative skills (two weeks), economics, government and the administrator (two weeks), principles of accounts (one week), the social role of government (three weeks), government and industry (three weeks), and international relations and United Kingdom interests (two weeks). Unless trained in those subjects previously, the fast-stream entrants would normally be expected to take the first three foundation courses, while there is no such expectation of the latter three, although most such entrants would seem likely to take the government and industry course, which includes a week's attachment to a private company. In about their fifth year, preferably as they are about to be promoted to principal, the fast-stream entrants can take a resource management course comprising three modules: staff management (two weeks), information as a resource (one week) and resource allocation and financial management (two weeks). All those courses are also available to the diplomatic service (grades DS8 and DS7).[34]

The fast-stream training scheme only involves a total of twenty-two weeks of central tuition (about half that which assistant principals had come to receive by the early days of the Civil Service College). Attendance at any or all of the courses is not mandatory, and there is a high rate of withdrawal from courses because of the demands of the work – it is usually work in a minister's private office. The Civil Service College has made intelligent use of the diminished resources available to it, which were always puny by ENA standards, but the clock does now seem to be turned back in the direction of the pre-CAS era. A new lease of life seems to have been given to the British belief that actually training for administrative work is inimical to virility. French administrative cadets, already well qualified in 'relevant' subjects, are required to undertake two and a half years of rigorous post-entry training, but British ATs, not normally equipped with 'relevant' degrees, are judged not to need to face such labours. French technocratic ambitions accord ill with British political traditions, but the aim of translating the ideal British administrator into the professional manager – an aim to which the Thatcher government subscribes, like Fulton before it – requires a substantial commitment to training. What sort of professionalism could it be which does not need extensive formal training? Together with the overwhelming reliance on decentralized recruitment, the chopping back on such central training provision as there was raises once more the question of the extent to which the civil service is, or should be, more than a collection of departmental staffs.

References

1 *Proposals for the Reform of the Foreign Service*, Cmd 6420 (1943), p. 2; *The Times*, 26 July 1967.
2 G. K. Fry, *Statesmen in Disguise* (London, 1969) pp. 56, 63, 429; H. E. Dale, *The Higher Civil Service of Great Britain*, (London, 1941), p. 16; *Report of the Royal Commission on the Civil Service* (Priestley Report), Cmd 9613 (1955), pp. 4, 84–91, *Report of the Committee on the Civil Service* (Fulton Report), Cmnd 3638 (1968), paras 192–243.
3 Fry, *Statesmen in Disguise*, pp. 39–42; *Interim Report of the Reorganization Committee* (1920–1); National Whitley Council Joint Committee on the Fulton Report, *Developments on Fulton* (1969), p. 28, and *The Shape of the Post-Fulton Civil Service* (1972), pp. 2, 5–10, 27–30.

4   *Civil Service Statistics 1982*, pp. 9, 21.

5   ibid., p. 21; *Chain of Command Review: The Open Structure. Report of a Team led by Sir Geoffrey Wardale* (Wardale Report) (1981), paras 2.1–2.3; information from MPO.

6   Wardale Report, 4.14, 5.12–5.22, 6.1, 6.2; *Civil Service Statistics 1972*, p. 18; *Civil Service Statistics 1980*, p. 23.

7   *House of Commons Weekly Hansard*, no. 1272 (1983), Written Answers, col. 236; CSD, *The Civil Service: Introductory Factual Memorandum Submitted to the House of Commons Treasury and Civil Service Committee* (1980), pp. 10–11; *Civil Service Statistics 1982*, pp. 21, 23.

8   Fulton Report, para. 215, pp. 163–5; Fry, *Statesmen in Disguise*, pp. 288–91; C. H. Sisson, 'The civil service – I. After Fulton, the pseudo-revolution', *Spectator*, 20 February 1971, p. 250.

9   *Report of the Committee on Representational Services Overseas* (Plowden Report), Cmnd 2276 (1964), paras 100–4. In diplomatic missions DS4s usually have the rank of counsellor, DS5s and DS6s of first secretary, DS7As and DS7Es of second secretary and DS8s of third secretary. Ministers are usually DS2 or DS3s but may occasionlly be DS4s. Ambassadors and high commissioners can be DS1s, DS2s or DS3s and sometimes DS4s (*Review of Overseas Representation. Report by the Central Policy Review Staff*, 1977, p. 442).

10   *Report of the Administration Trainee Review Committee* (1978), pp. 33–47, 56–62, 73–5; information from CSD.

11   H. J. Laski, *Reflections on the Constitution* (Manchester, 1951), pp. 182–4.

12   *Review of the Scientific Civil Service* (Holdgate Report), Cmnd 8032 (1980), pp. 42–4.

13   *Review of the Framework for Government Research and Development*, Cmnd 7499 (1979) p. 1; Holdgate Report, pp. 10–12, 16, 88, 135–6.

14   Fulton Report, p. 152; CSD, *Introductory Factual Memorandum*, pp. 11–13; *Framework for Government Research and Development*, Cmnd 5046 (1972), pp. 8–10; *Review of the Framework for Government Research and Development*, pp. 10–11; Holdgate Report, pp. 2–4, 26–7, 41–2, 50–1, 109–11, 116.

15   *The Use of Accountants in the Civil Service. Report of an Enquiry by Sir Ronald Melville and Sir Anthony Burney* (1973), pp. 7–10, 18–21; HC 535–II, pp. 625–6; *Extended Use of the Executive Class in the Civil Service. Interim Report of the National Whitley Council Committee on the Structure of the Post-War Civil Service, Treasury Circular 5/47, Whitley Bulletin*, March 1947, pp. 36–8; *CCSU Bulletin*, February 1983, pp. 26–9.

16   (Finniston) *Committee of Inquiry into the Engineering Profession. Co-ordinated Evidence of Departments employing Engineers in the Civil Service* (1978), p. 8; Holdgate Report, pp. 109–11.

17   W. A. Robson, 'The civil service and its critics', *Political Quarterly*, vol. 25 (1954), p. 300; Civil Service Commission, *Annual Report 1981* (1982), p. 11.

18   *Hansard*, vol. 773, HC Deb., 5s. col. 1547 (J. H. Wilson); *Sixth Report from the Estimates Committee. Recruitment to the Civil Service*, HC 308 (1964–5); K. M. Reader, *The Civil Service Commission 1855–1975*, Civil Service Studies no. 5 (1981), pp. 51, 55, 63–4, 69, 70, 71; *The Method II System of Selection. Report of the Committee of Inquiry* (Davies Report), Cmnd 4156 (1969), p. 82; Civil Service Commission, *Annual Report 1975* (1976), p. 7, and *Annual Report 1978* (1979), p. 8; Holdgate Report, p. 30.

19   F. H. Allen, 'The basis and organization of recruitment', *Management Services in Government*, vol. 36 (1981), pp. 21–8; Civil Service Commission, *Annual Report 1981* (1982), p. 11, and *Annual Report 1982* (1983), pp. 7–8, 19–30, 33.

20   Civil Service Commission, *Annual Report 1977* (1978), p. 8, *Annual Report 1979*, p. 8, and *Annual Report 1980* (1981), p. 8; Civil Service Commission, *Civil Service Recruitment of Graduates 1977–1979* (1980), pp. 7, 11–17; Civil Service Commission, *Annual Report 1982* (1983), pp. 9, 49, 54.

21   Civil Service Commission, *Civil Service Recruitment of Graduates 1977–1979*, p. 6; Civil Service Commission, *Annual Report 1982* (1983), pp. 8–9, 17–18, 54.

22   HC 535–I (1976–7), p. xviii; HC 535–II, pp. 472–6; HC 535–III, pp. 1090–5; Civil Service Commission, *Annual Report 1978* (1979), p. 50.

23   *Report of the Committee on the Selection Procedure for the Recruitment of Administration Trainees* (Allen Report) (1979), p. 2.

24 ibid., pp. 3–4; HC 535–I (1976–7), p. xxi.

25 Allen Report, pp. 2, 25, 26–7.

26 Civil Service Commission, *Follow-Up of the Administration Trainee Entry. Recruitment Research Unit Reports 3–6. A Covering Note* (1979), p. 4.

27 Allen Report, pp. 8–9.

28 HC 535–II (1976–7), p. 1090; Allen Report, pp. 4, 5, 16; Civil Service Commission, *Annual Report 1979* (1980), p. 8, *Annual Report 1980* (1981), p. 7, *Annual Report 1981* (1982), p. 9, and *Annual Report 1982* (1983), p. 9, information from FCO; *Review of Overseas Representation* (1977), p. 367.

29 *Selection of Fast Stream Graduate Entrants to the Home Civil Service, the Diplomatic Service and the Tax Inspectorate; and of Candidates from within the Service. Report by Sir Alec Atkinson* (1983), p. 6; Fulton Report, pp. 28, 162; *Review of Overseas Representation* (1977), p. 365.

30 W. A. Robson, 'Recent trends in public administration', in W. A. Robson (ed.), *The Civil Service in Britain and France* (London, 1956), p. 58; *Report of the Committee on the Training of Civil Servants* (Assheton Report), Cmd 6525 (1944), pp. 12, 16–18; *Twelfth Annual Report of the Civil Service College 1981–82* (1983), p. 7; C. H. Sisson, *The Spirit of British Administration*, 2nd edn (London, 1966), pp. xii, 29, 35–7.

31 A. Bertrand, 'The recruitment and training of higher civil servants in the United Kingdom and France', in Robson (ed.), *The Civil Service in Britain and France*, pp. 175, 179; T. Feyzioglu, 'The reforms of the French higher civil service since 1945 – I', *Public Administration*, vol. 33 (1955), p. 69; E. N. Suleiman, *Elites in French Society. The Politics of Survival* (Princeton, NJ, 1978), p. 41; E. N. Suleiman, *Politics, Power and Bureaucracy in France. The Administrative Elite* (Princeton, NJ, 1974), pp. 55–71, 88, 89–97.

32 Fulton Report, p. 135; A. Stevens, 'The *Ecole Nationale d'Administration*', in R. A. W. Rhodes (ed.), *Training in the Civil Service* (London, 1977), pp. 64–78.

33 C. D. E. Keeling, 'Treasury Centre for Administrative Studies', *Public Administration*, vol. 43 (1965), p. 191; *Report of the National Whitley Council Joint Committee on the Fulton Report. Fulton – The Reshaping of the Civil Service: Development during 1970* (Armstrong Report) (1971), p. 20; *The Civil Service Proposals and Opinions, Parts 1 and 2. Government Departments and Staff Associations. Evidence submitted to the Committee under the Chairmanship of Lord Fulton 1966–68*, vol. 5 (1), pp. 85, 86; Civil Service College, *Programme 1982–83* (1982), pp. 38, 239; *Civil Service Training. Report by R. N. Heaton and Sir Leslie Williams* (1974), p. 14; *The Times*, 11 November 1980.

34 *Eleventh Annual Report of the Civil Service College 1980–81* (1982), pp. 2, 8–9; Civil Service College, *Programme 1982–83*, pp. 11–30.

4 The Central Management of the Civil Service Question

1 'A Very Venerable Suggestion'

The central management of the civil service is involved with the allocation of money and resources to the service, and with the shape and manning of its career hierarchy. It is a role mainly performed at the core of the machinery of British government where the Cabinet Office and the Treasury meet; where an oversight is kept on that machinery, overall control of public expenditure is attempted and revenue collection organized, and macroeconomic management practised. With the exception of the diplomatic service which is run by the Foreign and Commonwealth Office and which has its own head, the central management of the civil service is the responsibility of the Treasury; one that, in only minor respects, it currently shares with the Management and Personnel Office, which is now part of the Cabinet Office structure.

The period 1968–81 when the central management of the civil service was assigned to the Civil Service Department (CSD) was an important exception to the rule of Treasury control. What was not exceptional was the idea that such management should be located away from the Treasury. 'It is a very venerable suggestion', Sir Warren Fisher told the Tomlin Commission in 1930 and one which, as he pointed out, the Haldane and Bradbury Committees had turned down in the past. Tomlin followed suit. This did not kill off the idea, for it had three important sources of life support. The first was from academics. Harold Laski was definite that 'a separation will have to take place between the financial and establishment functions of the Treasury. A separate Minister of Personnel is required to whom all questions of recruitment, training, promotion, pay and other conditions of service will be entrusted. The present fusion of functions in the Treasury has the undesirable result of making financial considerations unduly influential in personnel problems.' Laski said that the Treasury was 'not a creative but a critical department'. What it thought about 'first and foremost' was 'the saving of money'. Of course, that was why the civil service union movement – the second source of support – persistently agitated for the removal of establishment functions from the Treasury, in the hope of thus interposing a potential ally in the form of the new department between themselves and a known opponent in negotiations about pay and conditions. A third source of support for alternatives to Treasury control of the civil service was to be found among the civil servants themselves. At one level, the Treasury was bound to attract the kind of discontents about advancement that a clearly defined career hierarchy generates. So would any alternative, but this was easier to see after the change than before it. Rather more high-mindedly, some civil servants, along with others, did argue that in trying to run the civil service as well as controlling public expenditure and managing the economy, the Treasury was attempting to do too much. Some civil servants, as members of the Fabian group in 1964, favoured central establishment functions being taken over by a strengthened Civil Service Commission. This was another 'venerable suggestion', having been mooted, for instance, in Fabian circles twenty years before.[1]

Although reconstructured in the wake of the Plowden Report on the Control of Public Expenditure of 1961, the Treasury's prestige had been too diminished by its record in economic management for it to have much hope in the atmosphere of the 1960s of resisting the Fabian reformers and the unions' pressure for its establishment role to be moved elsewhere. Fulton fell for the idea and the CSD was born, to survive for thirteen years and a fortnight before overdue death. The cause of death was diagnosed by Sir Warren Fisher fifty years before: 'Let us look at this new institution with a Minister. He has got to square the Chancellor of the Exchequer; he cannot override the Chancellor of the Exchequer under the English Constitution. Then these Treasury officials come into play, so all you do is to make a much more cumbrous machine, with not a vestige of advantage to anybody.'[2] The unions continued to detect an advantage, but the Thatcher government determined to kill off the CSD. In the ensuing controversy, like the previous discussion, whether the type of central management that dated from the Fisher era was really needed now tended to be overlooked.

2 The Treasury and the Centre of British Government

Six major functions can be identified as being exercised at the centre of British government, as Sir Richard Clarke wrote in 1971. The first is the work of the Cabinet Office with its secretariat duties. The second is concerned with the machinery of government. The third involves the responsibility for the civil service. The fourth embraces central work on departments' organization, management and senior appointments. The fifth concerns the analysis, allocation and control of departments' objectives, expenditure and civil service manpower. The sixth involves management of the economy, finance and taxation. When it existed, the CSD performed the second, third and fourth functions, and shared the fifth with the Treasury. Setting aside the secretariat functions of the Cabinet Office – which the imperialistic Warren Fisher had tried, but failed, to bring within the Treasury in 1922 – the organization of the centre has generally been synonymous with the organization of the Treasury. The Treasury did coexist with a Minister for Economic Affairs presiding over an economic planning staff in the Cabinet Office in 1947, and with the Department of Economic Affairs between 1964 and 1969, and the CSD between 1968 and 1981. However, as an internal review observed in 1980, 'these examples of institutional separation appear as exceptions to the British administrative tradition'. The review also thought that 'the existence of a single comprehensive department' perhaps gave 'a misleading impression of integration at operational level'. Moreover, the Treasury has been frequently reorganized in attempts to cope with problems which have remained remarkably constant in character, if considerably different in complexity and scale.[3]

The classical Treasury organization existed before the First World War, when, aside from pensions and general financial matters, 'each Treasury division dealt, by departments, with every aspect of that department's activity – policy, supply control, complementing and pay'. This did not mean that the Treasury had the power to promote efficiency within the spending departments. Treasury control was 'confined to the negative', as Warren Fisher later put it, but not, as he said, because of lack of staff. Even if a more positive style of Treasury control of the kind advocated by the Playfair, Ridley and MacDonnell Commissions had been attempted, there was no way in which the departments of the time, still, in many cases, retaining the character of ministers' private offices, could be compelled to respond constructively. Nevertheless, in the commissions' urgings and accompanying structural proposals, there could be detected 'the germ of the idea that control of departmental expenditure on administration should be organized separately at the Centre from the control of expenditure'. The Haldane and Bradbury Committees took up the matter in 1918–19. Bradbury recommended 'the creation of a strong

Establishment branch in each department', and 'the creation of a central Establishments Division of the Treasury'. Bradbury believed that any other arrangement than location of central responsibility in the Treasury would entail 'friction and duplication of work'.[4]

The Treasury was reorganized in 1919. Much was made at the time about dispensing with the system which had grown up during the war of putting the headship of the Treasury into commission, and having one permanent secretary again. In fact, the 1919 structure, which was devised by the then Finance Committee of the Cabinet, made provision for no fewer than four officials of permanent secretary rank in the Treasury. It was then that Sir Warren Fisher was made permanent secretary to the Treasury and head of the civil service, including the Foreign Office, formally receiving in 1920 his controversially exercised powers to advise the Prime Minister on all the most senior appointments in other government departments, explicitly including those in the finance and establishment spheres. It was Fisher who founded the system of permanent secretaries acting as accounting officers for their departments. Fisher implied that the spirit of Gladstone was dead and that of the saving of 'candle ends' with it: there was much talk from him about team spirit and co-operation with other departments. The Staff Side of the National Whitley Council was less enthused and argued that, Treasury control of the civil service being 'unimaginative and destructive', what was needed was a new department under a Cabinet minister which would take over the Treasury's establishments role. The Tomlin Commission rejected the idea, being conscious of the 'overlapping' that would result. However, Tomlin did make proposals designed to encourage the Treasury to pay greater attention to organization and methods work and to the dissemination of developments to other departments. In practice, the Treasury's contribution in that area in the interwar period was later described by the Select Committee on National Expenditure in 1942 as being 'meagre in the extreme'. Nevertheless, that committee too turned down the idea of 'a new authority' at the centre because, given the Treasury's continuing responsibilities for the control of public expenditure, 'duplication and waste' might result.[5]

The appointment of the Geddes and the May Committees suggests that the interwar Treasury was not universally trusted even to effectively do its job of restraining public spending within cash limits, despite being backed by a public opinion whose dominant attitude was antipathetic to such spending. With support on the scale available, the methods of financial control did not need to be particularly sophisticated, and seem not to have been. 'That the

Treasury's control mechanisms never met the aspirations of its critics is not altogether surprising, given the resources available, and the continuing reluctance of departments to seek advice, or of the Treasury to make determined efforts to provide it' was the retrospective official verdict. Warren Fisher himself thought that the 1919 structure was 'an extremely unwieldy and top hampered and unsatisfactory arrangement'. Below him, and subject to his general supervision, and of a status comparable with permanent secretaries elsewhere in the service, there were three controllers presiding over what were indeed called departments within the Treasury for finance, establishments and supply services, with divisions beneath them. There was interchangeability of staff. The structure having been modified five years before, in 1932 the Treasury reverted to a divisional form of organization. 'The attempt in 1919 to impose a functional organization on a departmentally constructed set of divisions seems to have progressed so far, and then stopped. Meanwhile the top structure above the split was from time to time adjusted and readjusted.' An internal review later observed: 'that it worked at all may be due to the very small size of the undertaking and the relative importance of Establishments work'.[6]

The 1939 Treasury was a very small organization (about 400 staff, including subdepartments), and 'establishments work was the dominant, if less glamorous activity' at a time when 'the costs of the operations of central government still constituted a significant proportion of public expenditure and of the Government's total budget'. The Treasury and its subdepartments increased in size after that – to 1,150 staff in 1945, 1,700 in 1950 and 1,460 in 1960. By the 1960s from a position of broad equality in terms of senior staff before the war, the establishments side had dropped to being outnumbered by roughly two to one. Finance and supply had become the dominant Treasury activities, and it was later officially conceded that 'questions of efficiency in the Civil Service took a back seat'. What had dramatically changed the Treasury's role had been the assumption in the 1940s of the task of national economic management, which had imposed a wholly new load at the top of the department. Organizationally, the biggest change took place in 1947 when the statistical and administrative apparatus of national economic planning was brought into the Treasury. Generally though, 'the Treasury's fundamental structure in 1960 was recognizably that of 1940'.[7]

The Treasury of Sir Edward Bridges had a wider role than that of Sir Warren Fisher, except in the specific sense that, with the Foreign Office regaining its independence, Bridges himself could only act as head of the home civil service. Initially, from March 1945 Bridges combined that post and the headship of the Treasury with that of secretary to the Cabinet. In January 1947 Sir Norman Brook took over the Cabinet post. The Bridges Treasury was not without its controversies, sometimes as a result of guilt by association with failures in economic policy, but also because of Bridge's various declarations of faith in the all-rounder as the ideal administrator. There was less cause for friction than had existed before – despite Fisher's assurances – because of what Bridges called in 1950 'a trend away from meticulous control of detail in favour of greater delegation to departments, combined with the use of methods which will enable the Treasury to satisfy itself that the standards of prudent housekeeping are being observed'. Certainly, 'the traditional doctrine of Treasury authority for every new post or for every variation in establishment' had gone. That the establishment officer in departments was now an establishment and organization officer, paying more attention to organization and methods than before, and supported by the relevant teams and staff inspectors, was supposed to be a substitute. As for the Treasury's 'duty of prudent housekeeping', Bridges wrote that 'the heart of the business' was that

> the Treasury clerk is a layman dealing with experts; they will inevitably know more of their business than he can hope to acquire. But by dint of practice in weighing up facts, and testing evidence and judging men, it is his business to form a laymen's judgment on whether the case presented for expenditure, however admirable it may appear from a particular point of view, is out of scale with what can be allowed on a common sense judgment of things when other demands are taken into account.

The limitations of the layman approach, as well as the difficulties of greater financial freedom for departments, were illustrated in the progress of the Concorde project between 1956 and 1962. Anticipating the Treasury's likely scepticism about the costings and commercial viability of Concorde – based on sad experiences with military aircraft projects – the Ministry of Supply and then of Aviation managed to keep the Treasury out of the critical early stages of commitment. Unlike its French counterpart, the Treasury was even without a representative when the crucial treaty was drawn up. When the Treasury had the belated opportunity to stop Concorde, it was handicapped by its own lack of aviation expertise and a failure to use such experts as were available to it.[8]

'It really is an abuse of language to speak of a "system" of Treasury control', the Select Committee on Estimates observed in 1958, detecting the amateurish nature of the then arrangements. Thirty years after Fisher's assurances to the contrary, the committee still doubted if there was a real partnership between the Treasury and the departments in controlling spending. Although it attributed this to the persistence in the Treasury of the 'candle ends' philosophy rather than to departmental urges towards profligacy, of the kind that was present, for instance, in the Concorde venture. The committee recommended that a further investigation of Treasury control of expenditure was needed. The consequence was the Plowden Committee of 1959–61 and the Plowden 'revolution', as a result of which the arrangements for the control of public spending were drastically changed and the Treasury was reorganized. The system of annual cash limits on supply expenditure was pushed to one side. Plowden recommended that 'regular surveys should be made of public expenditure as a whole, over a period of years ahead, and in relation to prospective resources; decisions involving substantial future expenditure should be taken in the light of these surveys'. The surveys were undertaken by the Public Expenditure Survey Committee (PESC), chaired by a Treasury deputy secretary and including the principal finance officers of the major spending departments. Plowden implied that management had been relatively neglected in the service and said that this should be put right.[9]

The top of the Treasury had been reorganized as recently as 1956 when, on his retirement, Bridges had been replaced by two permanent secretaries. One of them, Sir Norman Brook, the secretary of the Cabinet, retained that post and combined it with the headship of the home civil service. The other, Sir Roger Makins, HM ambassador in Washington, took charge of the financial and economic work of the Treasury. Otherwise, the Treasury organization remained unchanged. There was another, this time more radical reorganization in 1962 in the wake of the Plowden recommendations and on the retirements of Brook and Sir Frank Lee (who had replaced Makins in 1960). Brook was replaced as secretary of the Cabinet by Sir Burke Trend. He was replaced as head of the service and joint permanent secretary to the Treasury by Sir Laurence Helsby. William Armstrong jumped from third secretary – deputy secretary elsewhere – to joint permanent secretary in place of Lee. Beneath Helsby and Armstrong there were, as before, three second secretaries – permanent secretaries elsewhere – two on the economic and financial 'side' and one on the management 'side'. Hence, in the top echelon of the Treasury, there were five permanent secretaries in all, the increased weight coming on the management 'side' where Helsby, as head of the service, concentrated his attention.

The Treasury was organized in five functional groups and two 'sides'. The management 'side' comprised pay and conditions of service, and management. The economic and financial 'side' comprised public sector (resources and expenditure), national economy, and finance. An internal review later commented:

. . .the 1962 reorganization abolished the mixed divisions and created a series of supply divisions responsible only for departmental expenditure; the separation between Supply and Establishment work (or 'management' as it had become known) which had been implicit in the 1919 structure was at last carried through to operational level. And at the very top of the official structure the distinction was recognized in the continuance of the Joint Permanent Secretary arrangements.[10]

Even a reorganization of this fairly substantial kind could not save the Treasury from its critics, the ranks of whom were made more numerous by failures in economic policy. An academic economist, Thomas Balogh, had earlier led the assault, advocating that the headship of the service be put into commission, and that the Treasury's role be split up in ways that would lead to the creation of a Ministry of the Budget and a Department of Economic Affairs (DEA). The latter institution was, of course, actually established by the Wilson government in 1964, the core being drawn from the national economy divisions of the Treasury. The DEA's role was bound up with long-term economic policy and the Treasury, still running short-term policy, inevitably prevailed. The DEA folded after five years in October 1969, the Treasury taking back what had been its to start with. Eleven months earlier, the Treasury had lost its establishment functions. The inheritor was not the Civil Service Commission, as, we have already noted, a Fabian group (incidentally including Balogh) had advocated in 1964. This was not least because the commission had come out poorly in a review conducted by the Select Committee on Estimates, in the very same report whose recommendations had paved the way for the appointment of the Fulton Committee. Fulton did take away the central management role from the Treasury and the Treasury divisions concerned went to form the core of the CSD. An internal review later tried to minimize the change that was represented by the CSD. It pointed out, for instance, that 'adjustments to the internal organization of the Treasury before 1968 never ran counter to the fundamental lines of functional division set up in 1919'; and that 'over the years the movement has been towards the complete separation between management and other functions at all official levels that was reached in 1962, and that was followed in 1968 by separation at Ministerial level'. The history of the organization of the centre was 'one of continuous readjustment of the administrative structure'.[11] Indeed, it was. Nevertheless, setting up the CSD was an important break with tradition. The Treasury had always been the central department with overall responsibility for the civil service. It was from the Treasury that Trevelyan, with the aid of Northcote, had reviewed the various departments. Proposals to supplement the Treasury's central role with other machinery – from Playfair and Ridley – had been resisted. MacDonnell, Haldane, Bradbury and Tomlin had all blocked proposals for supplanting the Treasury in civil service management. Establishing the CSD in 1968 was a departure. It also proved to be a mistake.

3   The Civil Service Department (CSD) Experiment

'The first main step in the reform of the Civil Service', the Fulton Committee said – and, hence, one which the Wilson government felt obliged to take – was 'the setting up of a new Civil Service Department'. This involved two important institutional changes. The Civil Service Commission was to 'cease to be a separate and independent organization'. It was absorbed into the CSD and, as Fulton proposed, a senior official there became first civil service commissioner. Even more important than this, of course, was that the Treasury was to be supplanted as the central department for the home civil service. Fulton's first argument in favour of this change was that the central management role needed to be enlarged especially as regards career development, and that 'if this enlarged responsibility' was 'added to the Treasury's responsibilities for financial and economic policy and for the control of public expenditure, there would be reason to fear too great a concentration of power in one department. The overall direction of the Service and the key to individual success within it should not both lie with the department that also uses the powerful weapon of central financial control.' Secondly, Fulton believed that the policy of interchanging staff between the two 'sides' of the Treasury, which meant that those engaged in central management tasks normally had their main training and experience in techniques of government finance and the control of expenditure, was an undesirable one. 'Full professionalism' demanded more specialization and, instead of Treasury predominance, for staff with experience in personnel management and organization in other government departments, and from outside the service too, to be brought in. Fulton also wanted departments to have delegated to them the maximum authority in staff and organization matters that was compatible with the requirements of the service as a whole. Thirdly, Fulton said that there could be no assurance that its reform programme for the service would be implemented in the 'radical spirit' necessary if central management remained with the Treasury. A 'separate institution' was needed and one which 'should be in the position to fight, and to be seen fighting, the Treasury on behalf of the Service'. As Fulton asserted that there was 'a lack of confidence in the Treasury' among civil servants, the hint was that 'a fresh start' would lead to better industrial relations. Under the post-Fulton dispensation, the Prime Minister remained First Lord of the Treasury but was also Minister for the Civil Service, the day-to-day responsibilities being delegated to a non-departmental Cabinet minister. The headship of the home civil service was transferred from the Treasury to the CSD.[12]

While the fact that the same permanent secretary continued to hold that headship minimized the appearance of the change, Sir William Armstrong was an enthusiastic advocate of setting up the CSD, as he emphasized twelve years later. He had even found the 1962 Treasury structure to be unsatisfactory. 'First, the management of the Civil Service inevitably brings with it a number of questions that concern not the Chancellor of the Exchequer but the Prime Minister.' Recommendations for Honours were 'a special matter': but two were

very closely linked with the normal duties of the CSD – machinery of government, because it is closely connected with the management services and organization and methods work of the department, and top appointments, because it is closely connected with the department's work on middle range appointments, especially the handling of 'fliers' and appointments to Under Secretary. If one man is to be responsible on these matters to the Prime Minister, while working on other Civil Service matters to the Chancellor he falls into the well known trap of serving two masters. In practice, he tends to turn his face towards the Prime Minister; the Chancellor senses this and resents it. From the Chancellor's point of view Civil Service work is inevitably a minor excrescence on his major preoccupation of framing and carrying out economic and financial policy. Time and again I saw some Civil Service crisis suddenly obtrude on the Chancellor, who was himself coping with urgent financial matters which, inevitably, seemed more insistent and more important. The result was that he turned to Civil Service matters with reluctance, scrambling through the meetings with the help of a brief, and left people feeling that his mind was on other things.

Second, came attitudes towards establishments work in the Treasury. Sir William said of the pre-CSD era that people came into the Treasury

> expecting to work on financial and economic matters – but the practice was to require people to work on both sides. A young man or woman with a background in economics would be dismayed to be told that the time had come 'to do your stint on Establishment' which is the way it was described in the old days. It was popularly regarded as equivalent to the salt mines or the galleys and the quality of the work, in spite of many heroic efforts, suffered accordingly.

Third, came a personal sentiment:

> I found it extremely irritating to be in charge of the Treasury financial and economic side – which is what most ordinary people think of as the Treasury – and yet not be in control of my own staff, since every move had to be agreed with my opposite number on the pay and management side. Although Sir Laurence Helsby was the soul of tact and friendliness, the fact remained that as Head of the Civil Service he could outgun me; and he frequently did.

It was these considerations, Sir William said – and which to the end of his life he believed held good – that led Fulton to recommend, and the government to accept, that 'the work of managing the Civil Service was of sufficient importance to be done by a separate department, brigaded neither with the Cabinet Office nor the Treasury, but coming directly under the Prime Minister with the appropriate ministerial assistance'.[13]

'The case for setting up the CSD at the time' of Fulton 'was absolutely overwhelming', Sir John Hunt, the secretary of the Cabinet, told the English Committee in 1977. In fact, Fulton's advocacy of the CSD, while dressed up in modern guise, was much the same as the time-worn arguments against Treasury control of the civil service that Tomlin had heard. Fulton never seriously met the arguments against change which Sir Lawrence Helsby presented in 1966. Fulton never seriously attempted to demonstrate what was wrong with Britain being 'almost alone' in giving its central finance department central managerial control over the civil service. For example, Australian experience of alternative arrangements was not encouraging. The case for the CSD never was overwhelming. Helsby demolished it, out-gunning Armstrong once more in argument. Inevitably, not all Helsby's points were of equal weight and he was perhaps at his weakest in dealing with the question of having a Minister for the Civil Service. Helsby pointed out that the historic structure of the Treasury meant that the Prime Minister as First Lord already had direct responsibility for such key aspects of civil service management as senior appointments and machinery of government. If there had to be another Minister for the Civil Service, the Financial Secretary to the Treasury would do. Politically, he would not, although Helsby was right when he predicted that a Cabinet minister with the task would 'either have very little to do or would find himself interfering in the management functions of his colleagues in relation to their departments'. As for the burden on the Chancellor, Helsby said that minister 'gives only the broadest policy attention to pay questions (and indeed would have to concern himself in the same broad way with pay policy even if the pay and management functions of the Treasury were transferred elsewhere)'. The crucial point, which killed off the opposing case intellectually, was that such was the size of the civil service salary, wage and pensions bill that the Chancellor had to have 'a major voice in decisions relating to so large a sector of public expenditure . . . the creation of a new Civil Service Department with a Finance and Public Sector Department retaining a strong interest in expenditure in the Civil Service would produce some duplication of effort'. In the sphere of management techniques, 'the dissemination of knowledge of these techniques, and their application to particular projects or blocks of expenditure call for close collaboration with the divisions dealing with expenditure, and the advantages of conducting such a joint operation in a single department are obvious'. Helsby recorded that 'the view is widely held among Permanent Secretaries that they prefer to deal with one central controlling department and fear that it would complicate their task of management to have to 'clear their lines' with two departments; that in particular the present system enables departments to get central approval of proposals as regards both staff and expenditure in the same operation, and they dislike the prospect of two independent, though overlapping, operations'. Helsby concluded that 'there can be no doubt that the change would be practicable if it were decided to make it, and it would offer some presentational advantage. On the other hand it might look like a bigger change than it was, and might give rise to expectations that problems too intractable to be solved by any Whitehall reshuffle would somehow vanish.' However, Helsby's arguments counted for little against those of the Royal Institute of Public Administration, assorted academics, the need to appease the civil service unions and the tide of fashion. Reshuffles and presentational advantages were the very stuff of the Wilson government of the 1960s, and so the CSD was born. [14]

As the 1962 structure had made the Treasury into what Sir Douglas Allen called 'a double-headed organization', the decision to set up two separate departments did not affect the problem of co-ordination in kind but· in degree. Nevertheless, as a Treasury official observed, 'where you have separate departments the problem of co-ordination is more difficult in the sense that more effort is required if the same degree of co-ordination is to be achieved'. Sir William Armstrong was told by colleagues that as long as he ran the CSD it would be all right because he would 'bring the power with you' – but 'what is going to happen when you are not there?' In the early days Sir John Hunt said

> the division worked pretty well . . . very largely because you hived off the management side of the Treasury into the CSD, and the people in the manpower departments and in the efficiency department were the old Treasury people. They knew their opposite numbers in the public expenditure divisions, they were used to working with them, and they had a lot of common experience. That is, inevitably, though no one's fault, a wasting asset, and you cannot go on running a department simply on old contacts. I think that the 'clout' of the CSD in part depended on the immediate post-Fulton programme and dynamism . . . and a department cannot for ever exist on the basis of one Report.

Sir Ian Bancroft's recollection, as the CSD's last permanent secretary, was that 'there was a period when the Department was first set up when it was concerned with two things basically. One was implementing Fulton and this carried along with it a zest and an exhilaration of its own and, two, with helping to plan the major machinery of government changes for 1970 which were in the pipeline . . . for some time'. Then, Bancroft was unclear, but Sir Douglas Allen thought in 1972, 'a pretty conscious decision was taken by the Government of the day . . . to draw a line under Fulton'. It was then that the CSD 'started taking much greater interest in the whole efficiency side of the operations' and, thereafter, that was 'the continuing theme'. Sir Ian believed that 'one has got to put the whole business of the drive for efficiency in historical perspective. The Centre, however constituted, has had a very important role in this regard for the last thirty years . . . I assert, because I was there, that the post-Fulton CSD has done more . . . than the pre-Fulton Treasury', although what was crucial was 'the approach of the Government of the day'. [15]

Sir William Armstrong had dwelt upon the difficulties that he had experienced inside the 1962 Treasury structure – which may have owed something to the personalities of the politicians and officials concerned – but what about the external difficulties which were bound to follow from the duplication inherent in establishing the CSD? Sir John Hunt's experience of the post-Fulton system was that 'departments tend to regard their battle as being with the Treasury and . . . having won that, they say "We have agreed to do this. Now let us go and get the manpower from the CSD"'. The CSD could not 'start the policy argument all over again'. Hunt's successor as secretary of the Cabinet, Sir Robert Armstrong, who initially believed the CSD to have been 'a good thing', later emphasized

> the disadvantages of separating control of supply expenditure from the control of manpower expenditure are real and I think that separation is a little illogical. In a sense, manpower is just one of the resources of which a government department disposes and there can be a trade-off between spending on manpower and spending on other resources. Certainly in the Home Office I was conscious of the illogicality of the separation from this point of view. During that time, and irrespective of the political complexion of the Government in power, the Treasury were at us to control our expenditure from the one side, and the CSD was at us to control our manpower from the other, and perhaps it felt a bit like being slugged from the left by one boxer and slugged from the right by another boxer, perhaps without the co-ordination of punches that one might have expected from a single pair of hands. Perhaps it made it a little easier to dodge the punches!

Sir Robert added that 'once you take manpower control and management into a separate department more effort is required if the same degree of co-ordination is to be achieved'. Sir John Hunt's experience had been similar:

> . . .we used to say that once policy had been settled, either in argument with the Treasury or by Ministers discussing an important matter collectively, the CSD could simply translate that into manpower expenditure. You got the grading right, and the numbers, you multiplied the staff by the salaries, and there it was. I think that life is not quite like that . . . I think that particularly when you come to the aspect of efficiency . . . there is a risk . . . of some aspects falling down the middle between the two departments. [16]

What about the belief that establishing the CSD would enhance the status of central management work? Sir Ian Bancroft recalled that one of the things that led as long ago as 1962 to separating the control of manpower and the management of the Civil Service from the rest of the Treasury's work was the feeling that in terms of Civil Service management you were doing a different sort of job. You were managing a human resource. You therefore needed people who tended to specialize in doing that . . . The whole business of coping with staff and trade unions does involve a little bit of expertise.

This was certainly the experience of Sir Douglas Wass, who served for three years in a pay division in what was in effect 'the CSD side of the Treasury'. When the split came, Sir Douglas – displaying the 'salt mines' and 'galleys' attitude recorded by Sir William Armstrong – was very happy that it occurred when he was 'on the right side of the iceberg', dealing with economic policy. Sir Douglas, the Treasury's permanent secretary 1974–83, agreed that criticism of the scale of resources put into man management by the 'old Treasury' was 'fair', but added that this did not make setting up the CSD a necessity. As Wass said, getting 'more people involved in training, more people in career development, a Civil Service College – all these things could have been done within a unified Treasury'. Indeed, they were being done under the 1962 Treasury structure: notably, the establishment of the Centre for Administrative Studies in 1963. Sir Douglas went further – and Sir Ian Bancroft agreed with him – in saying that there had been some loss in not being able to give the staff in the CSD 'the variety of work that a unified Treasury could'. Sir Douglas believed that 'though we have bred specialists in the CSD we may have overdone it in the sense that we do not now offer them what many of them would regard as the slightly more glamorous work of doing financial work . . . and economic work in the Treasury'. As Sir Ian concurred, it would seem that, while establishments work was no longer 'the Cinderella function' that Sir Douglas said that it had been in the pre-1962 Treasury, a separate department had not elevated it to Princess status. We have the testimony, too, of Sir Leo Pliatsky that while Sir William Armstrong 'applied himself with quiet enthusiasm to building up' the CSD, he soon 'hankered to be involved in economic policy' and, of course, became so involved. [17]

The question of overload if the Treasury was accorded central management functions as well as its other roles was a serious one. As Sir Douglas Allen pointed out:

. . . the responsibilities of the Treasury are very wide, and in terms of control over the economy or influence on the economy not only are

they very difficult and include dimensions which were not there in
1968, but they include the fact that as members of the EEC and of a
wider community there is now a constant need for travel by Treasury
Permanent Secretaries abroad. This was a burden which was not
there in the old days after the War when travel was quite limited. It
also means that there are more intellectual problems to be tackled
because the notion that we had in the fifties that it was very easy to
control the economy by the simple application of demand
management is no longer there. I think that if you inject the
additional responsibilities into the department, which will
presumably have a larger Treasury team, you will greatly add to the
burden of making the Treasury cohere.

Experience, however, had shown that even with the CSD in existence,
the Treasury, through its responsibilities for public spending, was
closely involved in central management tasks anyway. Should the CSD
be abolished and should the Treasury either wholly or partially take
over its functions then the staff concerned would be brought in too.
The understaffing of the Treasury in relation to its responsibilities
seems to be part of a tradition of trying to set an example to other
government departments and one which critics of the civil service
believe departments have a tradition of not following. The location of
central management functions elsewhere had not affected a rationalization of the Treasury, and the duplication that had resulted from
placing them outside that department had succeeded in making the
centre seem less coherent. As for the load on the Chancellor who, in
any case, had relevant responsibilities, retaining a Cabinet Minister for
the Civil Service would alleviate the burden. The civil service unions
made it clear that with such a minister they would not expect to see the
Chancellor and, even if they did, he did not have to see them. As Sir
Douglas Wass pointed out, the analogy was surely with the Chief
Secretary to the Treasury. Contrary to predictions, chancellors had
been successful in declining to act as a court of appeal from the chief
secretary.[18]
    The difficulties of the CSD swiftly making themselves evident, the
vultures soon began to gather in anticipation of it following the DEA
into the institutional graveyard. The first to show himself, in 1971,
was a former Treasury official, Sir Richard Clarke, one of the
architects of the administrative 'revolution' still going on at the time
and the high priest of the Plowden 'revolution' and of the PESC
system. Clarke, seemingly obsessed with creating large departments,
having run one in the Ministry of Technology, published speculations

about the structure of the centre which advanced a variety of ideas for change there – including a revived 1919 structure for the Treasury – none of which envisaged the continuance of the CSD in its existing form or, for that matter, in any form in which it was likely to develop. As early as 1972 the unions were worried about the CSD's prospects for survival in a Whitehall world of large departments. Nevertheless, the CSD persisted, surviving, for instance, the attentions of the English Committee in 1977. With the passing of the Fulton boom, that committee believed, the CSD had 'lost its *raison d'être*'. The committee's reconstruction proposals were modest enough – 'only the control of efficiency should be transferred to the Treasury' – but the Callaghan government chose to leave the CSD intact.[19]

What that government had already done was to take a big step back in the direction of restoring traditional Treasury control when, in 1976, it pushed the post-Plowden public expenditure planning system to one side, and emphasized control by annual cash limits. These limits were not simply applied to supply expenditure as before but – with the important exception of transfer payments – across the broad range of public spending. PESC's main author, Sir Richard Clarke, blamed its failures on inflation, saying that if prime ministers and chancellors were inflationists 'there is nothing to be done'. The reply to this was that with political opinion dominated by sentiments favourable to the expansion of public spending it was undermining of any sustained attempt at containment to have a public expenditure control system geared up to the future rather than the immediate situation, and based on what proved to be perennially optimistic projections of economic growth. Clarke subsequently wanted to incorporate 'long term programme examination of a much more searching character into the PESC system': but the PAR system introduced by the Heath government had been designed to do this and experienced such little success that it had to be abandoned in 1979. While cash limits were not easily reconciled with PESC, that was the system that emerged after 1976. From then onwards, relations between the centre and the departments on the control of public expenditure and the promotion of efficiency tended to change, culminating in the circulation of a concordat in May 1981, following a Treasury and CSD letter to permanent secretaries instructing them to bring their departments' internal audit procedures up to date. The concordat set out the respective roles of the centre and the departments and it was unexceptional stuff until it emphasized that, within the normal framework of their responsibilities to their minister, finance and establishments divisions in departments should ensure specifically that three things were done. First, 'that the Treasury or the CSD are consulted in advance on any new proposals outside the categories of delegated authority, or which would commit the Government to find resources additional to the agreed programme; and (under the Cabinet Office rules) before a paper is circulated to Cabinet or to a Cabinet Committee containing a proposal with expenditure or manpower implications'. Secondly, 'that the central departments are provided with any information needed for fulfilment of their responsibilities for allocation, control and central management'. Thirdly, 'more generally that central departments are consulted at a formative stage in policy discussions which could have substantial financial or manpower implications'.[20] This sounded like an attempt to reassert Treasury control in the traditional form. So why not re-establish the old, or at least the 1962, Treasury?

Having taken back in the core of the DEA in 1969, and having been reorganized in 1975, the Treasury by 1980 had the following shape. First, there were the central services – those provided by the establishments and organization group, the central unit, and the information division. Secondly, there was the chief economic adviser's sector which had 'general responsibility for macro-economic policy analysis, for forecasting the development of the economy, and for providing economic advice to the other sectors' as well as exercising a 'general oversight of the work of economists throughout the Treasury'. Thirdly, there was the overseas finance sector which was concerned with 'the balance of payments and exchange markets; the financial and economic aspects of EEC membership; and with the world financial and economic environment'. Fourthly, there was the domestic economy sector which was mainly concerned with macroeconomic policies including monetary, fiscal and industrial policy. Fifthly, there was the public services sector concerned with the planning, control and monitoring of public expenditure. Sixthly, there was the rating of government property department, staffed by specialist valuers, together with executive and clerical support staff, whose work follows from the fact that local rates are not payable on crown property and payments in lieu are made instead.[21]

From being a relatively small policy department in 1968, the CSD had by 1980 acquired a range of central executive and control tasks. At the outset, the CSD took over the Treasury's functions relating to pay and management of the service, and incorporated the Civil Service Commission. The CSD then took responsibility for the Civil Service College when it was set up in 1970, absorbing the Centre for Administrative Studies. In 1972 the Civil Service Catering

Organization (charmingly called CISCO and embracing previous central catering responsibilities) was set up in the CSD, and that department also took responsibility for the Chessington Computer Centre, which provided a payroll and staff record service both for it and sixty other departments. Also in 1972 the Central Computer Agency (CCA) was established in the CSD, bringing together the former management services (computer) division responsible for the financial control of adminstrative computer projects, HMSO's computer procurement division and central computer bureau, and the Department of Trade and Industry's technical support unit. In 1973 the CCA was made responsible for central policy on the provision and use of telecommunications for administrative purposes. Following the recommendations of the *Longer Term Review of Adminstrative Computing in Central Government,* the CCA was reorganized in 1980 and renamed the Central Computer and Telecommunications Agency (CCTA). The aim of the reorganization was to enable the CCTA to devote more attention to new technological developments and undertake regular reviews of the efficiency of computer systems; to extend consultancy services; to delegate small- and medium-value projects to the departments concerned; and to integrate telecommunications and computer work. The CCTA (with 736) and CISCO (with 1,850) employed between them about half of the CSD's 5,108 staff in early 1980. In the policy areas of the CSD, a succession of structural changes culminated in 1979 with the establishment of a functions and programmes command, which brought together the CSD's interests in the then recently launched Rayner scrutiny exercises.[22]

The institution of those exercises was evidence of the Thatcher government's belief that the CSD had not been doing its job in promoting efficiency and effectiveness in the civil service and evidence, too, that the CSD's days were numbered. In March 1980 the chairman of the House of Commons Treasury and Civil Service Committee wrote to the Prime Minister suggesting that the CSD had 'run out of steam' and asking for her views, which were that an investigation would be welcome. A subcommittee then conducted one and, from August 1980, an internal review was carried out, too. That review, like a memorandum submitted by the CSD and the Treasury, emphasized the virtues of the status quo. The review, for instance, made much of the fact that 'the 1081 staff of the Treasury are virtually all employed (common services only excepted) in advising on policy and have little or no direct responsibility for executive tasks', whereas 'less than one-eighth of the CSD's present manpower is involved in policy work comparable to that of the Treasury'. Such arguments, like others advanced, did not compare in weight, for example, with the Helsby catalogue. Nevertheless, the difficulties of change, which were spelt out by several witnesses, and the number of forms which it could take seemed to incline the committee against recasting the machinery of government. The Prime Minister, having encouraged the inquiry, seemed to feel bound by its findings and, first, in Parliament and, then, in a White Paper in February 1981, recorded her decision to leave things alone, if only for the present. Her adviser on efficiency, Sir Derek Rayner, one of the few witnesses to call outright for the CSD's demise, was blunt in his verdict: 'I've never known a business organization with two headquarters at opposite ends of the street. It's crazy.'[23]

The CSD's reprieve was bound to be temporary. While the CSD still had an empire – CISCO and the rest – plainly it had no distinctive role. As the flagship *Reform* in the 'Fulton' class, the CSD had been sunk some years before, although a number of optimistic reformers still wished to cling to the wreckage. Moreover, making the civil service as much like a business organization as practicable remained one of the Thatcher government's prime objectives. The CSD's apparent inclination to appease the unions during the civil service strike of 1981 ensured its death later that year. Mrs Thatcher – 'Madame Guillotine' according to *The Times* – acted as executioner:

> . . .setting up the Civil Service Department 13 years ago had a number of advantages compared with the situation as it existed before. But it had one consequence whose disadvantages have become increasingly apparent over time. It divorced central responsibility for the control of manpower from responsibility for the control of government expenditure. I judge that the balance of advantage now lies in favour of consolidating the CSD's manpower control responsibilities with the central allocation and control of all resources, and to make the Treasury responsible for control over Civil Service manpower, pay, superannuation, allowances and for the CCTA

and, she could have added, CISCO too. The staff concerned were transferred to the Treasury, as was the minister of state concerned, who would answer in the House of Commons for the whole range of civil service matters. The Prime Minister emphasized that

> it remains my view that there should not be a total merger of the Treasury and the CSD. The efficiency of the Civil Service in carrying

out its functions and the selection and development of civil servants are as important to the Government as the control of public expenditure. The machinery of government should make special provision for this, since it is a subject in which any Prime Minister is bound to take a close personal interest. I shall therefore continue to be Minister for the Civil Service and to be responsible for the organization, management and overall efficiency of the Home Civil Service and for policy on recruitment, training and other personnel management matters.

The Chancellor of the Duchy of Lancaster was to discharge these responsibilities on a day-to-day basis and to answer in the House of Lords for the whole range of civil service matters. Mrs Thatcher said that 'the staff involved in these functions will work alongside the Cabinet Office in a new Management and Personnel Office. Sir Robert Armstrong will be Permanent Secretary of this Office, and will also continue, as Secretary of the Cabinet, to head the Cabinet Office. He will be assisted on the business of the new office by a second Permanent Secretary.' The administrative changes dated from 16 November 1981 and – then came the sting in the tail of the announcement – they meant the early retirement of Sir Ian Bancroft and his second permanent secretary at the CSD, Sir John Herbecq. Bancroft was replaced by Robert Armstrong and the Treasury's Sir Douglas Wass as joint heads of the home civil service, with Armstrong continuing as sole head on the latter's retirement in April 1983.[24]

The civil service unions were predictably outraged. Their council commented:

> So, the CSD has gone. After 13 years of somewhat precarious existence, the CSD has been abolished and its functions distributed between the Treasury and the Cabinet Office. The CSD's last day of operation was, appropriately enough, Friday the 13th . . . With it, one must regretfully record, went the last vestiges of the Fulton Report – for . . . a return to the pre-Fulton regime is clearly envisaged. Nobody can seriously believe, for example, that the Treasury will be *more* generous on Civil Service pay. Equally, it is naive to believe that, in the quest for 'greater efficiency' (which really means stepping up the tempo for the galley-slaves) personnel management, as Fulton envisaged it, will get a look in. The possibility of a return to the Dark Ages is indicated, and nobody in the Civil Service should have any illusions about the implications.[25]

Certainly, there should have been no illusions about the implications of the perennial union agitation for the location of the central management of the civil service to be outside the Treasury. Although a certain type of reformer and/or academic had or chose to parade such illusions, the unions' position was always hard-headed. It remained, in essence, that expressed by W. J. Brown in 1918:

> What is necessary is that there should be set up a Board of Control for the Civil Service. This Board should take over all the functions now discharged by the Civil Service Commission, the staffing of all government departments, the fixing of rates of pay and conditions of service, the settling of general questions of promotion, and, generally, all matters relating to the recruitment and conditions of civil servants. This Board would be a separate department under a Minister of the Crown. It would present estimates to the Treasury in the same way as other departments, and would be subject to no other Treasury control than would be exercised in the scrutiny of the estimates.[26]

Pushing the Treasury to one side was clearly aimed at maximizing the likelihood of better pay days (as the Council of Civil Service Unions' comments on the death of the CSD implied). All the arguments for, and defences of, the CSD and suggestions as to how different things would have been if the core of the CSD had been formed from outsiders and not from Treasury officials, fall in the face of one massive hurdle – money. If there was to be central control of civil service manpower it had to go with the control of money in the Treasury, or risk duplication at the centre. Essentially, the 1981 changes restored Treasury control of the civil service, modified only by a kind of Public Service Commission in the form of the Management and Personnel Office (MPO). There seems little administrative logic in the division of work between the Treasury and the MPO, but the only change made so far was to bring the latter within the Cabinet Office in June 1983. Certainly, the CSD experiment was a superfluous essay in tinkering with the machinery of government. The post-Plowden Treasury, if not the pre-1962 one, was already pointed in the direction that the CSD was supposed to go. It may be the case now that what the unions – who seem to fear the break up of the civil service – call 'creeping departmentalism'[27] has gone too far for central management except of a broad kind.

References

1   Tomlin Evidence, 1. 18735; *Report of the Royal Commission on the Civil Service* (Tomlin Report), Cmd 3909 (1931), para. 590; H. J. Laski, 'Introduction', in J. P. W. Mallalieu, *Passed to You Please* (London, 1942), p. 11; H. J. Laski, 'The Tomlin Report on the civil service', *Political Quarterly*, vol. 2 (1931), p. 514; A Fabian Group, *The Administrators. The Reform of the Civil Service*, Fabian

Tract no. 355 (1964), pp. 32–6; A temporary civil servant (Evan Durbin), 'Post war machinery of government. III government administration and efficiency', *Political Quarterly*, vol. 15 (1944), pp. 103–4.

2　Tomlin Evidence, q. 18735.

3　Sir R. Clarke, *New Trends in Government,* Civil Service College Studies no. 1 (1971), p. 57; *The Integration of HM Treasury and the Civil Service Department. Report of the Study Team* (Hawtin–Moore Report) (1980), Annex 1, p. 1.

4　Hawtin–Moore Report, Annex 1, pp. 1–3; H. Roseveare, *The Treasury. The Evolution of a British Institution* (London, 1969), pp. 199–211; *First Report of the Civil Service Inquiry Commission* (Playfair Report) C 1113 (1875) p. 23; *Second Report of the Royal Commission on Civil Establishments* (Ridley Report), C 5545 (1888), pp. xi–xii; *Fourth {Majority} Report of the Royal Commission on the Civil Service* (MacDonnell Report), Cd 7338 (1914), p. 87; *Report of the Machinery of Government Committee* (Haldane Report), Cd 9230 (1918), p. 21; *Final Report of the Committee on the Organization and Staffing of Government Offices* (Bradbury Report), Cmd 62 (1919), pp. 4–5.

5　Sir T. L. Heath, *The Treasury* (London, 1927), p. 13; Sir H. P. Hamilton, 'Sir Warren Fisher and the public service', *Public Administration*, vol. 29 (1951), pp. 9–11, 17; *Statement Submitted to the Tomlin Commission by the Permanent Secretary to the Treasury*, p. 1270; Tomlin Report, paras 587–8, 590, 593, 595–7; *Sixteenth Report from the Select Committee on National Expenditure. Organization and Control of the Civil Service,* HC 120 (1941–2), paras 56, 98, 99.

6　Hamilton, 'Warren Fisher', p. 11; Hawtin–Moore Report, Annex 1, pp. 8, 11–12.

7　ibid., pp. 12–13.

8　Sir E. E. Bridges, *Treasury Control,* (London, 1950), pp. 21–2; P. Hall, *Great Planning Disasters* (London, 1980), pp. 88–94.

9　*Sixth Report from the Select Committee on Estimates. Treasury Control of Expenditure,* HC 254–I (1957–8), paras 94–5; *Control of Public Expenditure* (Plowden Report), Cmnd 1432 (1961), paras 12, 44.

10　*Hansard,* vol. 557 HC Deb., 5s. cols 635–638; vol. 664, HC Deb. 5s. cols 781–783; R. Clarke, 'The Plowden Report: II. The formulation of economic policy', *Public Administration,* vol. 41 (1963), pp. 21–2; Hawtin–Moore Report, Annex 1, p. 15.

11　T. Balogh, 'The apothesis of the dilettante: the establishment of mandarins', in H. S. Thomas (ed.), *The Establishment* (London, 1959), pp. 121–2; *Sixth Report from the Estimates Committee. Recruitment to the Civil Service,* HC 308 (1964–5); Hawtin–Moore Report, Annex 1, p. 21.

12　*Report of the Committee on the Civil Service* (Fulton Report), Cmnd 3638 (1968), pp. 79–80; *Hansard,* vol. 767 HC Deb., 5s., cols 455, 458.

13　*First Report from the Treasury and Civil Service Committee. The Future of the Civil Service Department,* HC 54 (1980–1), pp. 114–15; *The Times,* 8 July 1980.

14　*Eleventh Report from the Expenditure Committee. The Civil Service* (English Report), HC 535–II (1976–7), q. 1817; Fulton Report, p. 81; G. E. Gaiden, *Career Service. An Introduction to the History of Personnel Administration in the Commonwealth Public Service of Australia 1901–1961* (Melbourne, 1965), p. 433; *The Civil Service,* vol. 5, pt 1, *Proposals and Opinions. Parts 1 and 2. Government Departments and Staff Associations. Evidence submitted to the Committee under the Chairmanship of Lord Fulton 1966–68,* pp. 98–102; *Hansard,* vol. 767, HC Deb., 5s., cols 455, 458.

15　HC 535–II (1976–7), q. 34; ibid, q. 329 (F. Jones); ibid., q. 1485; ibid., q. 1817; HC 54 (1980–1), q. 1152; ibid., qq. 818, 867.

16　HC 535–II (1976–7), qq. 1817, 1823–4; HC 54 (1980–1), qq. 770, 789–90.

17　ibid., qq. 864, 897–90, 912, 932–4; Sir L. Pliatsky, *Getting and Spending* (Oxford, 1982), p. 109.

18　HC 54 (1980–1), qq. 903–4, 1123.

19　Clarke, *New Trends in Government,* pp. 37–71; *Whitley Bulletin,* January 1972, pp. 1–2; HC 535–I (1976–7), paras 74, 88; *The Civil Service. Government Observations on the Eleventh Report from the Expenditure Committee 1976–77,* HC 535, Cmnd 7117 (1978), p. 13.

20　*Cash Limits on Public Expenditure,* Cmnd 6440 (1976), pp. 2, 14–15; Sir R. Clark, *Public Expenditure, Management and Control. The Development of the Public Expenditure Survey Committee*

(London, 1978), pp. xi, 150, 158, 164; *The Times*, 27 May 1981; HM Treasury and CSD, *Control of Expenditure: Departmental Responsibilities*, May 1981, para. 20.

21 Hawtin–Moore Report, Working Paper 1, pp. 1–6.

22 ibid. Annex 1, pp. 19–20, and Working Paper 2, pp. 16–17; CSD, *The Civil Service: Introductory Factual Memorandum Submitted to the House of Commons Treasury and Civil Service Committee* (1980), p. 42.

23 HC 54 (1980–1), pp. xx and q. 770; Hawtin–Moore Report, pp. 5, 7–8; *House of Commons Weekly Hansard*, no. 1193 (1981), col. 1070; *The Future of the Civil Service Department. Government Observations on the First Report from the Treasury and Civil Service Committee, Session 1980–81*, HC 54, Cmnd 8170 (1981), para. 2; *Sunday Telegraph*, 1 February 1981.

24 *The Times*, 13 November 1981; *House of Commons Weekly Hansard*, no. 1221 (1981), pp. 658–9; *Guardian*, 22 December 1982.

25 *CCSU Bulletin*, December 1981, p. 153. It is interesting to note that the IPCS, the sole major union to oppose the establishment of the CSD at the time of Fulton (Evidence, vol. 5, pt 1, p. 292) did not maintain this opposition in 1981.

26 W. J. Brown, 'Service self-government', *Red Tape*, September 1918, p. 93.

27 HC 54 (1980–1), p. 63.

5 The Changing Civil Service Pay System

1 Principles of Civil Service Pay

'The Government does not consider that the pay of civil servants, or any other group, should be determined by the needs of individuals. Pay is a matter for the market place and social needs are the province of the social security system.' In saying this in evidence to the Civil Service Arbitration Tribunal in 1982, Peter Le Cheminant, then a deputy secretary in the Treasury, was expressing much the same sentiments as that department's Anderson Committee had done in 1923. These had been that 'in our view there is only one principle in which all the factors of responsibility, cost of living, marriage, children, social position, etc., are included — the employer should pay what is necessary to recruit and to retain an efficient staff'. Many economists and *The Economist* newspaper over the years have expressed similar sentiments. For they are in accord with the classical theory of wages which tells us that salaries, for instance, are 'the price of labour' and that 'in the absence of control they are determined like all prices by supply and demand'. Elements of 'control', however, are bound to be present in the non-industrial civil service which, conventionally, has almost entirely been a life career service to which many of the jobs done with its ranks are specific, notably on its generalist side, and movement out of which is further limited by pension conditions. Another obstruction to a market approach has been the fact that the civil service is heavily unionized, especially by white-collar standards. The perennial advice of *The Economist* to governments to 'follow the market' in determining civil service pay has tended to be only one of several suggested principles. So, we shall call it position A.[1]

Even in 1914, when market philosophy was supposed to be dominant in the world of economic ideas, the MacDonnell Commission said that it was 'an accepted principle with all parties that Government should be a "model employer"', despite it being believed that this made the state's operations more costly than those of private organizations. The commission particularly had in mind permanency of employment and pension rights. The notion of the 'fair wage' dates back at least to Tudor times, and the Fair Wages Resolution which passed the House of Commons in 1891 merely marked its modern revival. Its application to the industrial civil service was conceded in 1910 and confirmed in 1924. No such commitment was given to the non-industrial civil service: but the notion of the government setting an example has tended to recognize few boundaries, especially those set by money. Urgings on behalf of the lower paid in the service made to, and by one member of, the recent Megaw Committee took no account of financial constraints. In the same spirit, the Tomlin Commission of 1929–31 was unsuccessfully pressed by the Staff Side of the National Whitley Council and the Civil Service Clerical Association to make civil service pay rates specially favourable because the service was 'a highly selected class'. The Priestley Commission of 1953–5 was told that the civil service had 'the best negotiating machinery for clerical people', so it would be unfair to civil service clerks to make their pay comparable with outside clerks because the latter were inadequately organized. Priestley was also told that the outside rates for scientists were simply 'wrong' and that the civil service should 'give a lead' in establishing scientists' salaries at their 'right general level', meaning a higher one. This extreme version of the 'model employer' argument we shall call position B.[2]

A more modest form of the 'good employer' argument appealed to Priestley. This approach has been evident, for instance, in an award of the Industrial Court in 1927 which dealt with the pay of the manipulative classes of the Post Office, then in the civil service:

> in their consideration of the claims and counterclaims, the Court have taken the view that the broad principle which should be followed in determining the rate of wages of Post Office servants, is that of the maintenance of a fair relativity as between their wages and those in outside industries as a whole, and as between the various classes within the postal service, with due regard to the adequacy of the payment for the work done and the responsibilities undertaken.

Aside from the important matter of how the cost would be met, one problem with the 'fair relativity' principle was how to identify what it specifically meant in practical terms. A possible solution was to relate the civil service's pay increases to an outside index, either that of the cost of living or the wages index, as proposed, for example, by an alliance of the service's unions to Priestley,[3] and revised periodically afterwards in union circles, usually at times when the results of such an exercise seemed likely to be favourable. Priestley preferred a 'formula' of its own based on the principle that it was only 'fair' that civil service salaries should be at least comparable with those paid by the 'good employer' outside. Systematic indexation being ruled out, making the comparisons entailed the establishment of a special fact-finding machinery – notably, the Pay Research Unit. The 'Priestley formula' was not simply 'fair comparison': it was elaborated by provision for reference to internal relativities and for adjustments on the basis of interim movements in outside pay. Nevertheless, 'fair comparison' was the predominant element in the established arrangements for pay determination in the non-industrial home civil service between 1956 and 1980. 'Fair comparison' was 'fair relativity' by another name, and this more modest version of the 'model employer' principle we shall call position C.

That leaves the classic British compromise with the market – position D – which, as we shall see, the Megaw Committee adopted in 1982, as the Tomlin Commission essentially had done fifty years before.

2   The 'Tomlin Formula': A Compromise with the Market

'The basis of remuneration in the Civil Service should be such as is sufficient to recruit men appropriate to the particular duties and retain them in the Service without losing their keenness or efficiency.' In those terms, the market principle, position A on Civil Service pay, commended itself to the Tomlin Commission of 1929–31, which believed it to represent the 'true aim'. However, and without giving reasons, the commission also expressed the belief that the market principle did not necessarily indicate what a particular rate of pay should be. Unlike staff representatives at the time, the commission was satisfied that

> broad general comparisons between classes in the Service and outside
> occupations are possible and should be made. In effecting such
> comparisons the State should take a long view. Civil Service
> remuneration should reflect what may be described as the long term
> trend both in wage levels and in the economic condition of the country.
> We regard it as undesirable that the conditions of service of civil
> servants when under review should be related too closely to factors of a
> temporary or passing character.

Tomlin also said that civil service remuneration should display a 'fair relativity' with outside rates; and that it should be related, too, to changes in the cost of living. Hence, Tomlin compromised with the market by taking positions A and C at one and the same time. As *The Economist* said, the resulting 'Tomlin formula' was 'vague', and especially in the absence of an agreed means of ascertaining 'the facts' it provided a choice of grounds on which the staff associations could base their claims, and on which the Treasury could dispute them.[4]

A Royal Commission appointed in the same month as the Wall Street Crash and reporting a week or so before the May Economy Committee published its findings was almost bound to be affected by the severity of the contemporary economic climate. An economic blizzard was blowing outside a civil service which to the massed numbers trying to enter its ranks must have seemed a particularly comfortable haven in a world of high unemployment. The Tomlin Commission's disinclination to solely embrace the market principle suggested that it was not entirely a prisoner of the then rampant neo-classical economic orthodoxy. The only pay cuts which it recommended were for new entrants, and those as part of an abortive recommendation to introduce a contributory pension scheme into the service. Indeed, as a consequence of the commission's recommendations, a cost-of-living bonus dating from 1920 was consolidated into the basic scales of the lower grades and, broadly, at levels above those justified by the falling index. Given the surplus of potential entrants, there was a certain inevitability about the commission's conclusion that the pay of the broad mass of civil servants needed 'no substantial revision'. The economic situation inhibited the commission from recommending the immediate implementation of improved pay scales for the higher grades which it felt were justified. Tomlin thought that it would be wrong to stabilize the pay of such civil servants at existing levels for the rest of the decade, but that is what happened.[5]

'Notoriously Civil Service pay has lagged behind the rise in salaries in general, ludicrously so at the top' was the retrospective verdict even of *The Economist* on how the 'Tomlin formula' worked in practice. In fact, the relative deterioration in the salary position of the highest grades seems to have been part of a longer-term trend. A comparative exercise undertaken by Sir Charles Trevelyan in 1850 had shown that the highest ranking civil servants were generally less well renumerated than their counterparts in private institutions, although most markedly in kind rather than cash. The Asquith Committee in 1921, however, found that even after making allowance for security of tenure and pension privileges, when it took account of 'the emoluments of men holding comparable positions in the commercial and professional world or in the fighting services', it had to recommend that the 'century old rate of remuneration' for permanent secretaries needed to be increased in order to ensure that conditions of service were 'sufficiently attractive to secure an adequate supply of suitable recruits'. Even then, permanent secretaries' salaries were placed at a lower level than the committee had intended while, as hinted above, it was not until 1939 that Tomlin's recommendations for improved salaries for the higher grades were fully implemented. The Chorley Committee, reporting ten years later, said that 'in 1939 a substantial increase of salaries in the highest posts was overdue', and that in the meantime such increases as had been secured were 'a good deal smaller than those which had been granted, speaking generally, in other employments and in the lower grades of the Civil Service itself'. Chorley recommended increased salaries for under secretaries and above, and the improvements were made after delays justified by the 'economic condition of the country'. As Chorley said, the lower grades had fared rather better as a result of arbitration awards and the consolidation of bonuses into basic scales. Nevertheless, a well-known piece of contemporary research by Guy Routh showed that, although general wage rates had risen by more than 60 per cent between 1895 and 1950, over the same period the real salaries of most grades of civil servants had fallen. The researcher describes this situation as 'alarming', and others also seemed to find it so. It can be observed, however, that the period concerned is a long one and at the beginning of it even the simplest educational attainments such as one would expect, for example, of a clerk, would have greater relative market value than they were to have later. As the comparison was made with wage earners it can be pointed out that before the First World War civil servants not just of the highest grades could afford domestic servants, while between the two world wars almost all civil servants enjoyed security of tenure at a time of high unemployment. Civil servants normally worked shorter hours (except in the highest grades) and, moreover, usually worked them in much pleasanter surroundings. Civil servants generally benefited from comparatively much superior holiday, sick leave and pension arrangements. In addition, it would be a particularly unfortunate civil servant who did not secure some promotion in a life career. So that, even if salaries of particular grades in the civil service were relatively stagnant, an individual civil servant's pay would not necessarily similarly mark time and, also unlike wage earners, even the unpromoted civil servants (except those on the salary maximum) in most grades would receive annual pay increments. To take one example, whereas between 1947 and 1960 the average annual earnings of civil service executive officers as a class, as measured by the average of their pay scale, increased by only 97 per cent, by 1960 the average annual earnings of an individual executive officer who started working in 1947 at the age of 18 would have increased by 362 per cent, even if he had not been promoted to a higher grade. This was a rate of increase which few manual workers could match. Moreover, the much-maligned 'Tomlin formula' had been in force during most of the period concerned. None the less, with even *The Economist* lined up with its critics, by the mid-1950s that 'formula' was due for replacement.[6]

3   The 'Priestley Formula': The Elaborated Principle of 'Fair Comparison'

Whereas Tomlin had done its work in the depths of an economic depression, the Priestley Commission of 1953–5 reviewed civil service pay and conditions in the radically different economic climate of the Butler boom and the promise of a British 'economic miracle'. Keynesianism was the economic orthodoxy, inflation was low and the effects of full employment outside its ranks on the comparative advantages of a civil service career were beginning to be reflected in the recruitment statistics. To say that it was a different market, however, would be to fail to catch the mood of the times. For, as *The Economist* was soon to complain, 'a new lease of life' had been given in the 1950s to 'that amorphous but ancient concept, the fair wage'. The concept had been given some intellectual respectability in a book published in 1955 by Barbara Wootton, which poured scorn on the classical theory of wages and which advocated 'a rational wage policy', namely her own. Mrs Wootton was a member of the Priestley Commission and, to judge from the handling of the oral evidence, its ablest one. The Priestley doctrine of 'fair comparison' was along the lines that she advocated. While it noted how the civil service had increased in size in the meantime, Priestley acted as if it was designing a pay system for the smaller service of, say, 1939. How the government was supposed to meet the salary bills presented was not seen as a problem.[7]

Priestley was confident that it was earlier bodies such as Tomlin which had failed to get to 'the heart of the matter' of civil service pay. What needed to be aimed for, Priestley felt, was 'the maintenance of a Civil Service recognized as efficient and staffed by members whose remuneration and conditions of service are thought fair both by themselves and the community they serve'. The commission said that there could not be 'one short formula that can by itself solve all the wage and salary problems throughout the service'. Nevertheless, it did consider it possible to establish workable pay principles, and ones which would mean that civil service pay negotiations would not become involved with political issues and that would ensure that the non-political character of the service remained unimpaired. Priestley recommended that the 'primary principle' governing civil service pay should be 'fair comparison with the current remuneration of outside staffs employed on broadly comparable work, taking account of differences in other conditions of service'. For the broad mass of the service, the field of comparison should include both private and public employment. Priestley believed that, as far as comparisons with private industry and commerce were concerned, the larger undertakings would be the better guide because their size and structure made them more easily comparable with the civil service than smaller firms. Priestley said that in determining the pay of the higher civil service (which it took to mean those grades above principal) 'regard should be had to salaries in industry (private and nationalized), commerce and finance; to comparisons that can be made with other public services (for example, senior posts in the local authorities) and with senior university staffs; and to the level of remuneration which will be considered reasonable in the light of tradition and convention for the most senior civil servants'. The commission also indicated a 'secondary principle' that should govern civil service salaries, and that would serve as 'a useful and indeed necessary supplement to fair comparison', which was that account should be taken of internal pay relativities within the service. In addition, the commission recommended that in times of unusually marked and rapid movements in outside wages and salaries, adjustments should be made in the salaries of the lower and middle grades of the service by means of a central pay settlement. Such settlements were eventually (in 1970) made available to grades whose salaries did not exceed that of an assistant secretary.[8]

The 'Priestley formula' was not just distinctive because of its attempted comprehensiveness – 'fair comparison' plus internal relativities plus a form of occasional indexing – but also because 'the facts' were to be collected by machinery formally independent of government and intended to be permanent. The scope of this machinery was also fairly comprehensive. Excluded was the diplomatic service whose pay and conditions – which reflect the overseas commitment – remain along lines decided for it in the Plowden Report on that service of 1964. Excluded, too, in the home civil service were prison officers, whose pay remains determined along principles laid down in the Wynn–Parry Report of 1958. With these exceptions, the post-Priestley pay machinery, eventually modified, covered the bulk of the non-industrial civil service from the bottom to the top.[9]

For a decade and a half after Priestley, the continuing machinery reviewing higher civil service pay was provided by a small Standing Advisory Committee (SAC as had been proposed by Priestley at the suggestion of the Treasury. In comparing higher civil service pay with that of others, the committee, which was set up initially in February 1957, undertook reviews both on its own initiative and on that of the government, and generally followed the lines laid down for it by Priestley. Its reports, which were submitted directly to the Prime Minister (and only one of which was formally published), were not binding on the government but were generally accepted and implemented. In 1971 the SAC was disbanded. Its functions were taken over by the Review Body on Top Salaries (RBTS), which was appointed in May of that year under the chairmanship of Lord Boyle and then (from March 1981) of Lord Plowden. The RBTS not only advised the Prime Minister on the pay of higher civil servants (in the 'open structure' at under secretary level and above); but also made recommendations about the salaries of the higher judiciary, senior officers of the armed forces, MPs and the ministers of the crown. Until 1980 – when, at its own suggestion, its remit was changed – the RBTS made recommendations, too, about the salaries of the chairman and members of the boards of nationalized industries. Aided by management consultants and an advisory group, the RBTS drew its evidence on the wider basis suggested by Priestley rather than restricting itself to comparisons with industry, commerce and finance which the SAC had favoured. The RBTS was asked to undertake an immediate review following its appointment, and further reviews normally at two-yearly intervals. The first report affecting the pay of higher civil servants was published in June 1972, and it proposed substantial salary increases. This proved to be the pattern of the RBTS's findings which, predictably, were never published at times convenient for governments.[10]

Under the post-Priestley dispensation, the civil service Pay Research Unit (PRU) provided the main machinery which reviewed the salaries of the middle and lower ranks of the non-industrial civil service, meaning up to and including assistant secretary level. In contrast with later experience, for a long time the operations of the PRU were uncontroversial. Although *The Economist* soon labelled the PRU as 'perhaps the brightest jewel yet in the firmament of middle class bargaining', one more piece of evidence that 'few people in Britain are so well organized as civil servants to keep their pay up with the Joneses'. Priestley had recommended that in applying the principle of 'fair comparison' to the service a clear distinction should be made between negotiation and fact finding (meaning establishing job comparability and discovering the pay and conditions of service of jobs regarded as comparable), and that the latter activity should be assigned to a branch of the civil service not directly connected with the Treasury (later CSD) divisions responsible for pay and conditions. The PRU was duly established in October 1956 following the civil service National Whitley Council's acceptance of Priestley. The director was appointed by the Prime Minister and the PRU was controlled by a Steering Committee composed of members of both sides of the National Whiley Council. Until near the end of its life, the PRU was entirely staffed by seconded civil servants. What began as a five-year pay research cycle became a four-year one in 1964, a three-year one in 1967 and a two-year cycle in 1971. As by then it had been agreed that in alternate years there should be central pay settlements broadly related to the cost of living (only one of which, that of 1972, materialized) it was a short step in the adoption of an annual pay research cycle in the Pay Agreement of 1974. The annual pay research cycle consisted of three stages – fact finding, processing and negotiating. The fact-finding stage was begun with discussions between the PRU, the CSD and the unions about the pay research programme and the fields to be surveyed. The PRU then carried out an internal survey of civil service jobs, and an external survey of comparable jobs in outside firms. The PRU then completed its report on pay rates and other conditions of service for each job in each grade concerned. The PRU was then excluded from the remainder of the cycle. The second stage, that of processing, began when the CSD and the unions processed the information to produce adjusted true money rates thought to be properly comparable with civil service rates. The CSD and the unions then produced a list of rates to identify median rates for each grade as the basis of negotiation. That third stage began with the CSD and the unions negotiating over factors which could not be given a monetary value. Then the CSD wrote a submission setting out the implications of the evidence. Ministers then considered the submission and gave authorization for an offer. The CSD and the unions then engaged in final negotiations, and either reached a settlement or proceeded to the Civil Service Arbitration Tribunal.[11]

Whatever its beauties as fully developed, and however sophisticated language such as true money rates may have seemed – rather like the 'funny money' of the PESC system – the PRU cycle had the massive flaw that ministers were excluded from it until near its end. This was despite the scale of public expenditure involved in the pay of half a million civil servants – approximately £45 billion in 1982, for instance. It was at the point of implementation that the trouble usually started, and what the unions called 'government interference' occurred. One union leader, B. A. Gillman, complained in 1980:

> . . . only once . . . between 1964 and now have we been able to secure a PRU increase that has not been interfered with by Government. In 1968 the PRU increase was 'phased' by the Wilson Government, i.e. paid in two stages. In 1971, the time of the next PRU survey, there was no interference. In 1973, the Heath Government's statutory incomes policy meant that the increase due from January 1973 was deferred until November 1973. In 1975, the first year of operation of the new 1974 National Pay Agreement, which provided for annual pay reviews, Higher Executive Officers and above were denied by the Wilson Government the full benefit of the new uprating provisions. In 1976, 1977 and 1978 pay research was suspended by Government edict, and last year staging denied us the full increase from the due date. [12]

The details differed for grades other than those Gillman represented – essentially the former executive class – but the broad picture was much the same. Inevitably, governments were also given to 'interfering' with the implementation of the findings of the RBTS.

Civil service pay and conditions, which were normally only of much interest to the civil servants themselves and their unions, *The Economist* and a few academics, became the subject of mounting public criticism as the 1970s progressed and the economic situation deteriorated. When in 1971 the Heath government had introduced legislation providing for index-linked civil service pensions, for example, the measure had secured universal approval in the House of Commons – indeed, 'unqualified approval' from the Labour Opposition. Patrick Jenkin, the Conservative Financial Secretary to the Treasury, believed that 'our citizens will gladly shoulder the cost of meeting this obligation to those whose lives have been given to the Public Service'. He was proved wrong. Attitudes towards the civil service hardened as the artificial Barber boom gave way to real recession, and Keynesianism was replaced by a revived neo-classicalism as economic orthodoxy. By the mid-1970s *The Economist* was by no means alone in harbouring 'unkind suspicions that the Civil Service like the Devil, is most adept at looking after its own'. Although it led the way in characteristic style:

> At a time of soaring unemployment, you have almost total job security. You have just had a pay rise that drove a coach and horses

through the Social Contract. On top of your pay, now comparable with anything elsewhere you are promised, free, an inflation-proofed, final-salary-related pension that would require over a third of your annual salary to buy in the market. You are, of course, a civil servant. And what more could you want? Answer: your annual increment, which will enable you to drive another coach and horses through the pay-control policy you are about to apply to your fellow-citizens.

In fact, the application of incomes policy led to the suspension of pay research in 1976, the same year in which the PESC system was displaced by cash limits as the main means of attempting to contain the growth of public spending. Cash limits, if seriously and continuously applied, could act as a permanent form of incomes policy for civil servants and, as such, were incompatible with the Priestley dispensation, the operations of which had been already disturbed by more intermittent incomes policies. The English Committee of 1976–7, when reviewing the matter, contented itself with recommending that pay research should be restored and that, when it was, the PRU's work should be less cloaked in secrecy; its staff, including the director, should not be drawn exclusively from the civil service; and that supervision of the system needed to be undertaken by another and more independent body besides the Steering Committee of the National Whitley Council. These recommendations were accepted by the Callaghan government. In May 1978 a Civil Service Pay Research Unit Board was established 'with an independent chairman and members to safeguard the independence and impartiality of the Unit in all its work'. This invited the observation that once the 'impartiality of the 'unit' had to be so explicitly protected, it was doubtful if even an 'independent' board could inspire public confidence in pay research. Moreover, confidence was not the main problem. That was how governments could meet the bills which the PRU presented. In October 1980 the Thatcher government declined to do so, and abolished the PRU and its board. [13]

Priestley was dead. For the Thatcher government it was a merciful release. The actual facts about the pay of the main civil service groups in the Priestley era of 1956–80 are set out in Tables 5.1 to 5.4. [14] Far from ending controversy, statistics about civil service pay tend to fuel it. Treasury evidence to the Megaw Committee of 1981–2 suggested that civil servants pay was by then 5 per cent ahead of the pay of the private sector compared with their relative positions in 1970. Academic studies presented to Megaw concluded that there was little

Table 5.1   *Higher Civil Service Pay 1956–80*

Grade	1956 Royal Commission	1959 SAC £	1963 SAC £	1971 SAC £	1972 RBTS 2 £	1973 RBTS 3 £	1974 RBTS 4 £	1975 RBTS 6 £	1978 RBTS 10 £	1979 RBTS 11 £	1980 RBTS 14 £	% Increase 1980 of 1956
Permanent secretary to Treasury / Secretary to Cabinet / Head of home civil service	—	7,450	8,800	15,000	16,750	17,000	17,350	20,175	22,422	28,211	33,500	—
Permanent secretary	5,950	6,950	8,200	14,000	15,750	16,000	16,350	18,675	20,772	25,886	31,000	421·0
Second permanent secretary	—	—	7,700	13,000	14,750	15,000	15,350	17,175	19,122	23,811	28,500	—
Deputy secretary	4,200	4,950	5,800	9,000	10,500	10,750	11,100	14,000	15,629	20,314	24,500	483·3
Under secretary	3,350	3,750	4,700	6,750	8,250	8,500	9,000	12,000	13,429	16,714	20,500	511·9
Wages index (end of month)	Apr. 1956	Feb. 1959	Aug. 1963	Jan. 1971	Jan. 1972	Apr. 1973	Jan. 1974	Jan. 1975	Jan. 1978	Apr. 1979	Apr. 1980	
	105·0	116·6	134·5	213·8	238·9	279·2	306·9	396·5	590·07	721·05	853·04	712·4
Retail price index (mid-month)	102·7	110·3	121·0	172·7	186·8	207·6	225·4	270·3	427·07	482·74	587·75	472·3

Key: SAC = Standing Advisory Committee
RBTS = Review Body on Top Salaries, together with number of its Report

Source: Inquiry into Civil Service Pay: Research Reports. Report 2: Trends in Civil Service Pay Compared with other Indices submitted by HM Treasury, Cmnd 8590–I (1982), pp. 91–2.

Table 5.2 Administrative, Executive and Clerical Pay 1956–80

Grade	1956 Royal Commission £	1958 PRU £	1964 PRU £	1968 PRU £	1971 PRU £	1972 CPI £	1973 PRU £	1974 GPI £	1975 PRU £	1978 GPI £	1.4.79 PRU £	1.8.79 PRU £	1.1.80 PRU £	7.5.80 PRU £	% Increase 7.5.80 of 1956
Assistant secretary	2,600	3,350	4,300	4,950	6,300	7,276	8,500	8,850	11,000	12,273	13,378	13,991	17,000	19,500	650·0
Senior principal (SCEO)	2,000	2,650	3,300	4,000	5,200	5,200	5,564	6,700	9,350	10,809	11,782	12,322	15,000	17,500	775·0
Principal	1,850	2,325	2,900	3,425	4,400	4,708	5,425	5,775	7,450	8,729	9,515	9,951	11,750	14,000	656·8
Senior executive officer	1,442	1,800	2,250	2,720	3,400	3,638	4,245	4,542	5,900	7,032	7,665	8,016	8,900	10,500	628·2
Higher executive officer	1,158	1,375	1,750	2,100	2,625	2,809	3,350	3,585	4,700	5,718	6,233	6,519	7,250	8,555	638·8
Executive officer	990	1,110	1,360	1,610	2,000	2,150	2,600	2,782	3,670	4,579	5,043	5,272	5,700	6,745	581·3
Clerical officer	660	765	935	1,100	1,385	1,489	1,760	1,883	2,540	3,280	3,627	3,791	4,000	4,740	618·2
Wages index (end of month)	Mar. 1956	Oct. 1958	Dec. 1963	Dec. 1967	Dec. 1970	Dec. 1971	Apr. 1973	Jan. 1974	Apr. 1975	Apr. 1978	Apr. 1979	Aug. 1979	Jan. 1980	May 1980	
	103·7	115·9	137·7	163·7	210·6	236·6	279·2	306·9	421·9	644·7	721·1	748·8	830·6	860·8	730·1
Retail price index (mid-month)	101·3	109·4	122·4	142·4	170·4	185·8	207·6	225·4	290·9	438·6	482·7	520·4	552·8	593·2	485·6

Key: PRU = Civil Service Pay Research Settlement
      CPI = Central Pay Increase
      GPI = General Pay Increase

Source: For Tables 5.2, 5.3 and 5.4, G. K. Fry, 'Civil service salaries in the post-Priestley era 1956–1972', *Public Administration*, vol. 50 (1972), pp. 319–33, with additional information from the CSD.

Table 5.3 Scientific Civil Service Pay 1956–80

Grade	1956 Royal Commission £	1958 PRU £	1961 PRU £	1964 Admin. conseq. £	1968 Admin. conseq. £	1971 PRU merged £	1972 CPS £	1973 GPI £	1974 GPI £	1975 Admin. conseq. £	1978 GPI £	1.4.79 PRU Admin. conseq. £	1.8.79 PRU Admin. conseq. £	1.1.80 PRU Admin. conseq. £	% Increase 1.1.80 of 1956
Principal scientific officer	1,850	2,325	2,418	2,900	3,425	3,425	4,100	5,200	5,550	7,205	8,461	9,222	9,646	11,343	513·1
Senior scientific officer	1,265	1,590	1,654	2,012	2,372	3,355	3,483	4,150	4,441	5,778	6,898	7,519	7,864	8,705	611·9
Higher scientific officer (until 1.1.71 experimental officer)	1,075	1,285	1,336	1,618	1,910	2,350	2,515	3,150	3,371	4,454	5,448	5,938	6,211	6,737	526·7
Scientific officer	1,001	1,175	1,222	1,470	1,740	1,900	2,043	2,500	2,675	3,527	4,415	4,865	5,085	5,486	448·1
Assistant scientific officer (until 1.1.71) scientific assistant	605	695	780	920	1,100	1,395	1,500	1,775	1,899	2,560	3,303	3,652	3,818	4,030	566·1
Wages index (end of month)	March 1956 103·7	Oct. 1958 115.9	Jan. 1961 123·5	Dec. 1963 137·7	Dec. 1967 163·7	Dec. 1970 210·6	Dec. 1971 236·6	Nov. 1973 300·6	Jan. 1974 306·9	Apr. 1975 421·9	Apr. 1978 644·7	Apr. 1979 721·1	Aug. 1979 748·8	Jan. 1980 830·6	700·9
Retail price index (mid-month)	101·3	109·4	112·3	122·4	142·4	170·4	185·8	219·5	225·4	290·9	438·6	482·7	520·4	552·8	445·7

Key: Admin. conseq. = Administrative consequential.

Table 5.4 Professional and Technical Pay 1956–80

Grade	1956 Royal Commission £	1958 PRU £	1965 PRU £	1969 PRU £	1971 CPS £	1972 PRU £	1973 PRU £	1974 PRU £	1975 PRU £	1978 GPI £	1.4.79 PRU £	1.8.79 PRU £	1.1.80 PRU £	7.5.80 PRU £	7.5.80 % Increase 7.5.80 of 1956 £
Principal professional technology officer (Senior grade until 1.1.72)	1,850	2,300	3,000	3,625	4,208	4,760	4,900	5,850	7,450	8,729	9,515	9,951	11,021	13,200	613·5
Professional and technology officer I (Main grade until 1.1.72)	1,540	1,875	2,425	2,925	3,396	3,760	3,923	4,198	5,930	7,064	7,700	8,053	8,601	10,200	562·3
Professional and technology officer II (Basic grade until 1.1.72)	1,130	1,375	1,830	2,225	2,583	2,910	3,062	3,611	4,720	5,739	6,256	6,542	6,901	8,100	616·8
Professional and technology officer III (Leading draughtsman until 1.1.72)	880	1,115	1,430	1,790	2,227	2,390	2,538	2,993	3,925	4,869	5,307	5,551	5,820	6,900	684·1
Professional and technology officer IV (Basic draughtsman until 1.1.72)	746	955	1,220	1,550	1,999	2,090	2,226	2,625	3,450	4,326	4,768	4,984	5,253	6,300	744·5
	Apr. 1956	Nov. 1958	June 1965	Dec. 1968	Dec. 1970	Dec. 1971	Apr. 1973	Jan. 1974	Apr. 1975	Apr. 1978	Apr. 1979	Aug. 1979	Jan. 1980	May 1980	
Wages index (end of month)	105·0	116·1	145·7	173·3	210·6	236·6	279·2	306·9	421·9	644·7	721·1	748·8	830·6	860·8	719·8
Retail price index (mid-month)	102·7	109·8	132·4	150·9	170·4	185·8	207·6	225·4	290·9	438·6	482·7	520·4	552·8	593·2	477·6

relative change in civil service pay compared with that in the private sector between 1956 and 1970; but that between 1970 and 1980 the civil service had gone ahead by either 0·5 per cent or 0·25 per cent, depending on which academic one followed. The margin of error was 2 per cent on either side. The present writer's earlier research, known to Megaw, showed that between 1956 and 1972, the members of the majority of the main civil service grades subject to pay research generally did well in terms of salary, increases compared with one measure of outside movements of pay, the wages index. This research also demonstrated that the lower grades on the generalist side of the service fared less well. Taking the period 1956–80 as a whole, Tables 5.1 to 5.4 show that it was the exceptional grade (that, since 1972, called professional and technology officer IV, in fact) which had bettered the wages index. This suggests that, at least from 1972 onwards, using the same measure, the main part of the civil service lost ground in terms of relative pay. Megaw chose to play it safe, concluding that since 1956 'movements in overall Civil Service earnings appear to be very broadly in step with movements in private sector earnings'. The *Financial Times*, for one, translated this as meaning that 'the despised pay research system actually did the job it was supposed to do, keep Civil Service pay broadly in line with pay outside the Service'.[15]

Such sentiments understated the case against the Priestley dispensation, as well as interpreting the 'Priestley formula' narrowly. All the statistics represent are the bare facts, which are subject, as we have seen, to several interpretations, and which can only give a static and partial view of civil service pay and conditions over the period 1956–80. In fact, the period was a dynamic one, particularly in the sense that during it the non-industrial home civil service grew substantially in size. In the context of such expansion, it would be an unusually unfortunate established civil servant who did not secure a promotion or even promotions and, hence, more pay, whatever happened to basic rates. Moreover, although staff inspection was supposed to rule it out, expansion also made ascent up the promotion ladder more likely in the form of 'grade drift' which critics believed compensated the service for what the unions portrayed as the discriminating impact on it of incomes policies. Such policies never extended to civil service increments. One of the unsung achievements of the unions during this period was to secure shortened incremental scales. For instance, in 1956, the clerical officer and executive officers scales were 21 and 20 points in length respectively. By 1980 the clerical officer scale had been reduced to age points between 16 and 20, and a main scale of 6 points; and the executive officer scale was down to age points between 18 and 20 plus only 4 points. The bare statistics, dealing with salary maxima, did not record the financial benefits for the individual civil servants concerned of having few incremental rungs to climb on scales which in most years were moving in an upwards direction anyway. [16]

Some civil servants also benefited from the fact that the 'Priestley formula' was not just one of 'fair comparison with outside pay' – part of it enabled reference to be made to internal relativities. By such reference, for example, the Institution of Professional Civil Servants (IPCS) was able to 'avoid pay research' in 1964 and 1968, and still secure salary increases for the scientists it represented by establishing pay relationships with the administrative class which had been subject to such research. When the IPCS was 'forced unwillingly into pay research' in 1971, it was not surprised when the PRU's findings were 'unsatisfactory'. The evidence showed that, whereas the salaries of the lowest grades of scientist in the civil service should be increased, those in most grades ought to be reduced, in some cases substantially. The IPCS then went to arbitration and accepted the verdict of the Tribunal, while describing it as 'a perverse award'. From another perspective, it did seem to be, because the award's implementation meant that those grades which pay research suggested should have their salaries cut had secured a 5 per cent increase. In the meantime, the IPCS organized what was then the biggest rally of its members in its history to protest against the settlement. Its journal recorded that 'the strength of feeling was most clearly shown by the two gallant scientists who cycled 300 miles from Cumberland to attend the main London meeting'. Such ritual protests could not obscure the fact that, although Priestley had been clear that for the service to 'give a lead' on pay was 'incompatible with the principle of fair comparison', the application of the internal relativities part of its 'formula' in this instance, at least for a time, left many members of the scientific civil service better paid than their supposed 'analogues' in the private sector. [17]

In important respects, of course, conditions in the private sector were not analogous and, as the economic situation deteriorated, that sector's spokesmen were prominent among the numerous critics of civil service 'privileges' in general, and of the PRU in particular. The civil service unions pointed out to Megaw that 'civil servants receive a basic salary with no additional entitlement to company cars, free or cheap meals, assisted housing and the like', and cited evidence that the provision of such fringe benefits in the private sector was not only widespread but growing. In the context of contemporary trends in the

1970s and early 1980s towards rising inflation and unemployment, however, the security of tenure and the index-linked pensions of civil servants could be seen as the best fringe benefits of all. In 1980 the union leader, W. L. Kendall, having written to *The Times* saying that cuts in the civil service made job security there a sick joke, had to concede under questioning before a House of Commons Committee that there had been no redundancies in the service at a time when unemployment was increasing rapidly outside. The unions' defence of index-linked pensions tended to rest on two main points. One was that, although the civil service pension scheme was formally non-contributory, civil servants paid for their pensions on the form of adjustments to salary scales designed to meet half the cost. While this was informative, the fact remained that, commercially, index-linked pensions were, literally, something that money could not buy. The unions' other main point was to emphasize that civil servants accounted for only about one-seventh of those receiving public sector index-linked pensions. National health service employees (including doctors and nurses), policemen and firemen, members of the armed forces, judges, MPs and ministers, and local government and university employees (including teachers) received them too, and so did some employees of nationalized industries by analogy. This was informative, too, but it did not deal with the position of relative advantage enjoyed in relation to the private sector. The Thatcher government appointed the Scott Committee of 1980–1 to sort the matter out, but to the government's chagrin and to the delight of the unions, the committee evaded the issue by suggesting that the way out of the situation in which in pension terms there were 'two nations' – one indexed and one not – was for everybody to have inflation-proofed pensions. Unsurprisingly, the Scott Committee was unable to show convincingly how the private sector in general could finance such an open-ended commitment. The committee did hint that civil servants might well be paying too little for their pension rights, but it only recommended modestly increased notional contributions. After the Scott fiasco, the government had little choice about letting the pensions matter rest at least for the immediate future. Nevertheless, the fact remains that the changes made in superannuation arrangements in the 1970s represented 'revolutionary improvements in the conditions of employment of civil servants' – in the words of one union general secretary – and that this offset any tendency that there may have been for the service to 'fall behind' supposed outside 'analogues' in strict salary terms.[18]

The Priestley dispensation came under intense attack from the mid-1970s onwards. The fire was sometimes general in aim and, at other times, directed against the specific target of the PRU which came to be portrayed as anything but disinterested. *The Times* caught the mood in 1977:

> It is bad enough that civil servants themselves decide which jobs in industry and commerce are analogous to those in the Civil Service. It is worse that they draw their comparisons solely from those firms which are closest in structure to the Civil Service, i.e. companies like ICI, Shell, BP, Unilever, and the big banks and insurance companies. These are inevitably also the best paid. British civil servants thus enjoy a ratchet system which in normal times ensures that their salaries are linked to those in the most efficient sectors of British industry and commerce – even though they work, generally speaking, in more congenial and less hazardous circumstances, and are much less accountable for the results of their decisions than businessmen.

That the PRU had been following the guidelines laid down by Priestley tended to be ignored. The Confederation of British Industry (CBI) emphasized the point about large companies constituting an unfairly generous source of outside comparisons in its evidence to Megaw. The PRU's findings could also be said to take insufficient account of differences in conditions of service. The Clegg Comparability Commission, which worked closely with the PRU, admitted in 1980, for example, that it did not know of any instance in which security of tenure had been quantified in pay negotiations.[19] In the economic situation which had developed by 1980, pay arrangements which treated virtual immunity from redundancy as not affecting salary determination were no longer sufficiently widely politically acceptable either to be seen as 'fair' or to survive. The advantages of the Priestley dispensation to civil servants had always been evident to those excluded, even if, from time to time, the unions had urged the merits of form of indexing. 'Imagine our critics now if we had both index-linked pensions and index-linked pay', one union official wryly remarked in 1980.[20] Of course one can only imagine it, because no government could afford the arrangement for long. This brings us to the heart of the problem and to why pay research, although a cheaper arrangement than index-linked pay, had to be finally abandoned. Given the size and cost of the modern civil service, Priestley's ambition of placing that service's pay arrangements 'outside politics' was an unrealistic one. So, there can be little surprise that – as the 'Gillman catalogue' indicated – it was the exceptional period when the Priestley system worked in the manner intended. However easy it was for the Eden government to make the commitment to Priestley in 1956, its successors increasingly found it difficult to meet the cost of the resulting public expenditure. The Thatcher government, facing a similar situation, abolished pay research and its machinery and crushed the inevitable strike, towards the end of which it appointed the Megaw Committee to devise different and, it must have hoped, less costly arrangements and ones more subject to systematic political control.

4 The Megaw Report of 1982: A Compromise with the Market Again?

In June 1981 the Thatcher government appointed a committee comprising Sir John Megaw, a retired Lord Justice of Appeal, as chairman, and eight others, with the following terms of reference:

> Having regard to the public interest in the recruitment and maintenance of an efficient and fairly remunerated Civil Service and in the orderly conduct of the business of Government and its services to the public; to the need for the Government to reconcile its responsibilities for the control of public expenditure and its responsibilities as an employer; to the need for good industrial relations in the Civil Service; and to recent experience of operating the existing arrangements for determining the pay of the non-industrial Civil Service: to consider and make recommendations on the principles and the system by which the remuneration of the non-industrial Civil Service should be determined, taking into account other conditions of service and other matters related to pay, including management, structure, recruitment and grading.[21]

The Megaw Committee presented its findings in July 1982. There were in fact two reports – a Majority Report and a Minority one – the latter being submitted by John Chalmers, a former general secretary of the Amalgamated Society of Boilermakers and member of the TUC General Council.

That there was a division in the Megaw ranks should not have been as surprising as the Majority seemed to find it. Divisions over civil service pay are essentially concerned with attitudes towards public money and the Megaw divisions were no exception. Mr Chalmers, in the minority, argued for the 'model employer' approach, especially its extreme version, position B. He wanted exemplary treatment of the low paid, with the staged introduction into the civil service of a minimum wage as proposed by the service's unions in their evidence. This would involve a 'very modest cost', although Chalmers did not indicate the amount or, for that matter, the consequences for civil service numbers. Were there to be still more cuts and if not, how would the sums concerned be raised? He seemed to believe that he had settled the question, instead of begging it, by insisting that cash limits should be set after pay negotiations had been completed. Chalmers wanted to build on the Priestley system which, he said, had 'worked well', although it had eventually broken down because of 'persistent and worsening breaches' of it 'by successive Governments'. The question, of course, is why governments had acted in this way? The answer is because they could not find the money, whereas Chalmers (like Priestley) believed that the money can always be found.[22]

The Megaw Majority was not so sure, although it did not go to the other extreme and endorse position A – the Anderson/Le Cheminant/ market approach, which some thought summed up the Thatcher government's approach too. In fact, Megaw was told that

> the Government recognizes that comparisons with outside rates of pay and conditions of service in comparable employment provide a useful broad indication of what is required for these purposes. Comparability in some form plays a part in pay negotiation in the public and private sector alike. Accurate information about the labour market is a valuable management tool particularly for an employer like the Civil Service which has to recruit and retain a very wide range of employees in a wide variety of locations with different skills, aptitudes and qualification.

Megaw also found that comparisons played an important part in determining pay in foreign civil services. So the scene was set for the Majority to take position D – the classic British compromise – dressed up in contemporary clothes, some of them designed by Rayner from Marks and Spencer. The Megaw Majority recommended that 'the governing principle for the Civil Service pay system in the future should be to ensure that the Government as an employer pays civil servants enough, taking one year with another, to recruit, retain and motivate them to perform efficiently the duties required of them at an appropriate level of competence'. In accordance with this principle

> Civil Service pay increases and levels of remuneration, including fringe benefits, should in the longer term broadly match those

available in the private sector for staff undertaking jobs with comparable job weight . . . The main comparisons used in the system would be the trends of percentage increases in comparator pay rates in the current pay round. This information would be supplemented as soon as possible, and thereafter every fourth year, as a check, by information on levels of total remuneration . . . the data collection and analysis would be carried out under the supervision of an independent Board.

This Civil Service Pay Information Board was to comprise five 'independent minded persons' appointed by the Prime Minister; and 'to maintain demonstrable independence from the Civil Service management and the unions, surveys, data collection and analyses should be undertaken by management consultants on behalf of the Board'.[23]

What the Majority called 'informed collective bargaining' was to begin when the board provided the negotiating parties with its findings. The limits within which a pay settlement could be reached would be 'the inter-quartile range', meaning the middle ranges of outside pay. Management needs were to be given due weight, although the Majority emphasized that 'the Government should regularly make clear, as it has done to us, that the cash limit system does not necessarily imply a completely rigid control of pay increases on the basis of the initial assumptions'. The Majority wanted greater importance placed on internal relativities than under Priestley, involving discussions of them between management and the unions against the background, where relevant, of job evaluation. The Majority recommended that the Civil Service Arbitration Agreement should be renegotiated to give the unions the same right as the government to refuse to go to arbitration; with agreement to submit, ideally, binding both parties to accept the findings. The Majority favoured 'arrangements to encourage more active departmental and line management needs and efficiency, and measures to relate performance directly to pay'. Incremental scales were only to be retained for grades below principal and equivalent, and even then related to performance as measured in annual reports. For grades from principal to under secretary level, incremental scales should be replaced by merit ranges, again on the basis of annual reports. The pay of civil servants at under secretary level and above should continue to be settled without negotiation, after the receipt of the RBTS's reports. The Majority believed that governments should more readily implement the RBTS's recommendations than in the past, the financial cost being normally small. As for index-linked pensions, the Majority did not attempt to duplicate the Scott Report; but it did say that civil servants' pension contributions should be made more explicit.[24]

It is relatively easy to challenge some of the details of the Megaw Majority Report. For example, the political cost of implementing the RBTS's findings is likely to be disproportionate. It certainly seemed so in 1982 in the midst of the health service strike. All governments have to try to contain public sector pay, and giving ground at the top is not usually thought to be the most effective way to do this. As for merit pay, perhaps few would challenge this Raynerite ambition in principle and who would not wish to see the annual reporting system improved? How to do it is the problem. If there is to be some kind of appeals procedure – as the Minority suggested – what real incentive will the reporting officer have not to aim for the safety of the middle of the reporting range? Even this may be optimistic, to judge from evidence about annual reports submitted to Megaw. This found that, in different parts of the service, a range of between 40 and 75 per cent were reported as being either 'outstanding, exceptionally effective' or 'very good'; between 20 and 50 per cent were 'good'; between 5 and 10 per cent were 'fair'; and a mere 1 per cent were either 'not quite adequate' or 'unsatisfactory'. Stopping increments would be one way of penalizing the less competent: but identification would have to be swift given the brevity of some of the scales now. A further emphasis on accelerated promotion would give the changed arrangements a more positive appearance: but it is difficult not to believe that, for most of the service, Buggins's Turn will remain dominant. As for its suggested pay arrangements in general, the Majority's proposed 'catching up exercise' every four years risks all the old problems that retrospective PRU rises used to make for in any particular year. Regarding the composition of the Pay Information Board, some dread can be expressed about just who the 'independent minded' members are to be. The privatization of the fact-finding machinery, as *The Economist* called it, was probably inevitable after the long campaign led by that journal to discredit the PRU. Ironically, *The Economist* did not think that management consultants eager to retain a contract would be much more 'independent'. Given that the civil service has long since ceased to be primarily metropolitan in location, it is difficult to see why the Majority, trying to give greater emphasis to market forces, rejected regional pay.[25]

The Megaw Majority's findings resemble a sophisticated version of the 'Tomlin formula', with a similar emphasis on the market, modified by outside comparisons, but with developed fact-finding machinery – a compromise with the market. These findings seem to offer something for everybody, but most of all something for the government. For the unions, cash limits are not to be too constrictive and arbitration is to be on a more equal basis. This is no mean asset, for the Arbitration Tribunal's 'split the difference' recommendations on the 1982 pay claim are a reminder that the spirit of Harold Laski still lives on there. A greater stress on internal relativities than before offers other opportunities – notably for specialist groups – to advance claims. There are also the 'catching up exercises'. Moreover, the pay comparisons are potentially generous, for the unions are not confined to the bottom end of the market: they will be able to roam over 'the inter-quartile range'. Nevertheless, the 'Tomlin formula' was kinder to the taxpayer than the Priestley one. It remains to be seen whether the Megaw findings will have this effect and are similarly durable. The initial union reaction to Megaw was a wary and often hostile one. The unions' Council, for instance, tended to agree with the assessment made by Aubrey Jones, formerly of the National Board for Prices and Incomes: 'It is a pity that the inquiry did not forthrightly state that the Public Service should not be used to depress pay elsewhere. A statement to that effect would have done much to abate trade union criticism. Worse, much of its thinking is shallow. A successor to the Priestley Report of 1955, it will be seen by history as greatly inferior to Priestley in thinking.[26] The Priestley Report, of course, is notorious rather than famous in the eyes of those who share the Thatcher government's philosophy and at present there seems no way of knowing what the verdict of 'history' will be on Megaw. Its 'thinking' seems in no way 'inferior to Priestley'. Both reports are creatures of their time. From the Thatcher government's point of view, the prime achievement of the Megaw Majority was that it endorsed the dismantling of the Priestley system under which, in effect, the PRU, a body independent of the elected government, had decided the size of a substantial block of public expenditure – an arrangement which successive governments had found unworkable.

References

1   *The Economist*, 24 April 1982, p. 38; *Report of the Committee on the Pay etc, of State Servants* (Anderson Report) (1923), p. 4; J. R. Hicks, *The Theory of Wages* (Oxford, 1932), p. 1.
2   *Fourth {Majority} Report of the Royal Commission on the Civil Service* (MacDonnell Report), Cd 7338 (1914), p. 83; B. Bercusson, *Fair Wages Resolutions* (London, 1978), pp. 3–228; P. B. Beaumont, *Government as Employer – Setting an Example?* (London, 1981), pp. 9–14, 27–50; Tomlin Evidence, qq. 6004–6; *Report of the Royal Commission on the Civil Service* (Tomlin Report), Cmd 3909 (1931), para. 303; (Priestley) *Royal Commission on the Civil Service 1953–55. Minutes of Evidence*, qq. 599–600, 1847–50.

3   Tomlin Report, para. 301; Priestley Evidence, p. 11 (Civil Service Alliance).

4   Tomlin Report, paras 304, 307, 344; *The Economist*, 26 November 1955, p. 726.

5   Tomlin Report, paras 309, 317, 328–74, 697–778; B. V Humphreys, *Clerical Unions in the Civil Service* (Oxford, 1958), pp. 170–4.

6   *The Economist*, 26 November 1955, p. 726; *Papers respecting the Emoluments of Persons in the Permanent Employment of the Government* (1856); J. D. Rimington, 'Some observations on the salary of permanent secretaries', *Public Administration*, vol. 60 (1982), pp. 471–81; *Report of the Committee on the Salaries of the Principal Posts in the Civil Service* (Asquith Report), Cmd 1188 (1921), para. 4; *Report of the Committee on Higher Civil Service Remuneration* (Chorley Report), Cmd 7635 (1949), paras 7–8, 21, 25; G. Routh, 'Civil service pay 1875 to 1950', *Economica*, n.s., vol. 21 (1954), pp. 201–23; Humphreys, *Clerical Unions*, pp. 194–212; G. S. Bain, *The Growth of White Collar Unionism* (Oxford, 1970), p. 59.

7   *The Economist*, 16 July 1960, p. 261; G. Williams, 'The myth of "fair" wages', *Economic Journal*, vol. 66 (1956), pp. 621–34; B. H. Wootton, *The Social Foundations of Wage Policy* (London, 1955), pp. 11–27, 161–90.

8   Priestley Report, paras 87, 95–6, 99, 116, 145, 147, 366, 769 (42); *Whitley Bulletin*, November 1970, p. 161.

9   *Report of the Committee on Representational Services Overseas* (Plowden Report), Cmnd 2276 (1964), paras 441–603; *Report of the Committee on Remuneration and Conditions of Service of Certain Grades in the Prison Service* (Wynn-Parry Report), Cmnd 544 (1958), para. 98; *Report of the Civil Service Pay Research Unit 1979*, p. 12.

10   Priestley Report, para. 384; Priestley Evidence, qq. 3185–95; National Board for Prices and Incomes, Report no. 11, *Pay of the Higher Civil Service*, Cmnd 2282 (1966); Review Body on Top Salaries, Report no. 2, Cmnd 5001 (1972), pp. 10, 13; Review Body on Top Salaries, Report no. 6, Cmnd 5846 (1974), pp. 20–2, Review Body on Top Salaries, Report no. 14, Cmnd 7952 (1980), pp. 2–3; *House of Commons Weekly Hansard*, no. 1179 (1980), cols 33–4, and no. 1203 (1983), col. 220.

11   *The Economist*, 16 July 1960, p. 261; Priestley Report, paras 136, 139; HC 535–II (1976–7), pp. 7013; CSD, *Civil Service Pay: Factual Background Memorandum on the Non-Industrial Civil Service submitted to the Megaw Committee* (1981), pp. 28–31; *Report of the Civil Service Pay Research Unit 1968*, paras 23–5; *Report of the Civil Service Pay Research Unit 1969*, paras 2–9; *Report of the Civil Service Pay Research Unit 1971*, para. 5; *Report of the Civil Service Pay Research Unit 1979*, p. 21.

12   *Opinion*, January 1980, p. 1.

13   *Hansard*, vol. 818, HC Deb. 5s. cols 252, 293; *The Economist*, 4 January 1975, p. 57, and 26 July 1975, p. 67; HC 535–I (1976–7), pp. xxviii–xxx; *The Civil Service. Government Observations on the Eleventh Report from the Expenditure Committee Session 1976–77*, HC 535, Cmnd 7117 (1978), pp. 10–11; *Report of the Civil Service Pay Research Unit 1979*, p. 1.

14   In Table 5.1, salaries shown for 1956 are for intermediate centres (i.e., London salaries with a £50 deduction); from 1959 onwards 'national' rates are shown. For Tables 5.2, 5.3 and 5.4 there are no entries for 1976 and 1977 as there was no increase in basic pay in those years. In 1976 a supplement was payable of £4.00 per week for those aged 16 and under, £5.00 per week for those aged 17, and £6·00 per week for all others earning less than £8,500. In 1977 an additional supplement was payable to all non-industrial civil servants. The supplement was 5 per cent of total earnings subject to a maximum of £4·00 per week and minima of £1·95 per week for those aged 16, £2·15 per week for those aged 17, and £2·50 for those aged 18 or over. For Tables 5.2, 5.3 and 5.4 provincial rates are given.

15   *{Majority} Report of the Inquiry into Civil Service Pay* (Megaw Report), Cmnd 8590 (1982), paras 49–55; Megaw Report, Vol. 2: *Research Studies*, Cmnd 8590–I (1982), pp. 70–169; G. K. Fry, 'Civil service salaries in the post-Priestley era 1956–1972', *Public Administration*, vol. 32 (1974), pp. 331–3; P. Bassett, 'Civil service pay – the facts', *Financial Times*, 15 July 1982, p. 21.

16   Priestley Report, paras 463, 490; *Whitley Bulletin*, June 1980, p. 96.

17   *State Service*, September 1971, p. 257, and October 1971, p. 289; Priestley Report, para. 99.

18   *CCSU Bulletin*, January/February 1982, pp. 20–1; *The Times*, 5 November 1980; HC 54

(1980–1), q. 1111; *Whitley Bulletin,* April 1980, p. 55; R. Hemming, 'Estimating the value of a civil servant's indexed pension', *Fiscal Studies,* vol. 1 (1980), pp. 49–55; *Report of the Inquiry into the Value of Pensions* (Scott Report), Cmnd 8147 (1981), pp. 7, 20–1; *Annual Report of the Institution of Professional Civil Servants 1972,* p. 21 (*State Service,* March 1973).

19   *The Times,* 6 October 1977; CBI Evidence to Megaw, November, 1981, pp. 12–14; Standing Commission on Pay Comparability, *Report No. 9,* Cmnd 7995 (1980), p. 26.

20   *Whitley Bulletin,* December 1980, p. 173 (P. D. Jones). An agreement was actually reached on 22 December 1960 which provided for an annual trigger for civil service pay based upon the index of weekly wages. This agreement was put to the civil service unions' annual conference in 1961 and, following rejection by the then UPW, it was also rejected by the then CSCA. As a result of this, the agreement was never ratified by the National Staff Side (*Whitley Bulletin,* February 1961, pp. 21–2; information from P. D. Jones 15 February 1981).

21   *House of Commons Weekly Hansard,* no. 1213 (1981), col. 577.

22   Megaw Minority Report, pp. 103, 105, 107, 115, 116.

23   HM Treasury, *Civil Service Pay. Government Evidence. Submitted to the Inquiry into Non-Industrial Home Civil Service Pay under the Chairmanship of Sir John Megaw* (1982), para. 6; Megaw Majority Report, paras 91, 101, 111, 112, 125, 128, 129.

24   ibid., paras 98, 102–4, 163–4, 195, 219, 269–70, 335, 339, 344, 355, 359–60.

25   ibid., para. 339; Megaw Minority Report, pp. 104, 116; *House of Commons Weekly Hansard,* no. 1264 (1983), Written Answers, col. 22; *The Economist,* 10 July 1982, p. 21.

26   *Observer,* 11 July 1982; *CCSU Bulletin,* August 1982, p. 145; J. Gretton and A. Harrison (eds), *How Much Are Public Servants Worth?* (Oxford, 1982), pp. 93–101.

6 The Changing Character of Civil Service Unionism

1 The Trojan Horses

When the Civil Service National Whitley Council celebrated its golden anniversary in 1969, it seemed natural that it should do so in 'a blaze of self-congratulation', as the journal of the employees, or Staff Side, ten years later described the proceedings. 'Civil Service industrial relations were put forward as a model for other industries. The prized Whitley system seemed to be set nicely for another fifty years of proud development.' However, by the end of the 1970s, the Staff Side believed that Whitleyism was 'in a pretty parlous state'. That decade had seen 'the Civil Service drift into a situation in which its industrial relations have become amongst the worst in the country. Ten years ago direct action by civil servants was virtually unheard of – now it is a common feature, and not merely on pay issues. Civil servants have readily embraced a militancy in their attitudes towards employment issues that was unthinkable ten years ago.' In fact, in 1969, in the same year as Whitleyism's fiftieth anniversary, the Civil Service Clerical Association, the largest union in the service, had adopted a strike policy supported by a fighting fund. *Staff Relations in the Civil Service* – to follow the title of the relevant official handbook – were being translated into industrial relations of an earthier kind. The first civil service strike took place in 1973 over pay. A more prolonged strike campaign in 1979, also over pay, saw the unions force the Callaghan government into surrender. Severe differences with the Thatcher government over pay, and over manpower cuts, led the unions to conduct a five-month strike campaign in 1981 which resulted in a government victory. These strikes were important, for they demonstrated that many civil servants, as represented by their largely professionalized trade union movement, were prepared to act aggressively if what they deemed their self-interest was frustrated by governments; to act as if the civil service was an independent entity in the state. Whereas old-style Whitleyism was plainly compatible with British constitutional practice, militant civil service unionism consciously and inevitably directed against elected government could not be. Indeed, by acting in a spirit of militant confrontation quite alien to Whitleyism, and entering into arrangements for co-ordinated action, the civil service unions were well described by their traditional foe, *The Economist*, as behaving like Trojan horses.[1]

2 The Civil Service Unions and the Whitley System of Joint Consultation

While the civil service unions have forced themselves into a form of public prominence, few outside the ranks of the non-industrial civil service probably realize that it is highly unionized compared with many areas of employment. Union membership is about 80 per cent. By the early 1980s mergers since 1968 had reduced the number of major unions from 27 to 9. Table 6.1 lists these unions, giving their membership totals in the late 1970s and in brackets their membership in the civil service and 'near fringe' departments – meaning such bodies as the Forestry Commission, the Metropolitan Police and Museums; but not public corporations such as the Post Office, the Atomic Energy Authority and the British Airports Authority. Adding together the figures, it is evident that in the late 1970s the civil service unions had a total membership of 589,866, of whom 523,424 were drawn from the civil service and 'near fringe' departments.[2]

Table 6.1   *Membership Total of the Civil Service Union in the late 1970s*

Union	Membership	
Association of First Division Civil Servants (FDA)	5,706	(5,706)
Association of Government Supervisors and Radio Officers (AGSRO)	12,043	(9,682)
Association of Her Majesty's Inspectors of Taxes (AIT)	2,518	(2,518)
Civil and Public Services Association (CPSA)	224,780	(184,684)
Civil Service Union (CSU)	46,827	(45,732)
Inland Revenue Staff Federation (IRSF)	67,614	(67,614)
Institution of Professional Civil Servants (IPCS)	103,342	(90,305)
Prison Officers' Association (POA)	22,189	(22,189)
Society of Civil and Public Servants (SCPS)	104,847	(99,994)

Plainly, the unions differ considerably in size. The largest, the Civil and Public Services Association (CPSA) is the old Civil Service Clerical Association (CSCA) under a different name since 1969; the union making the change because it retained its membership in the Post Office when, in that year, that institution was converted into a public corporation. In the civil service, the CPSA represents the clerical officer, clerical assistant, DHSS local officer 2, secretarial, data processing and teleprinting grades, as well as some departmental grades in the Lord Chancellor's Department and the Ministry of Defence. The change in status of the Post Office, and the retention of membership there, similarly led the Society of Civil Servants (SCS) to translate itself into the Society of Civil and Public Servants (SCPS) in 1976. In the civil service, the SCPS represents the various executive grades. The Institution of Professional Civil Servants (IPCS) represents the specialists meaning, for instance, members of the professional and technology group, the science group, the professional accountant class and medical officer class as well as many other general service groups and classes and the members of some of 250 departmental classes. The Inland Revenue Staff Federation (IRSF) represents the taxes grades, the collector grades and the Valuation Office staff of the Board of Inland Revenue. The Civil Service Union (CSU) represents cleaners, messengers, officekeepers, paperkeepers, security officers and telephonists, as well as various specialist grades including uniformed members of the coastguard service and state foresters. The members of the Association of Government Supervisors and Radio Officers (AGSRO) are employed in Ministry of Defence establishments. The Prison Officers Association (POA) represents the uniformed members of the prison service. The tiny Association of Inspectors of Taxes (AIT) represents HM inspectors of taxes, and works closely with the First Division Association (FDA) except where its more specialized interests are under consideration. While the FDA shares recognition with the SCPS for some of the lower grades, broadly it can be said to represent the old administrative class area of the service, together with all grades in the legal category, the economist group, the statistician group and the HM inspectorate of schools. The FDA has links with the Diplomatic Service Association.[3]

All but one of the unions employ professional trade unionists to help to run their affairs. The exception is the AIT, which still relies on serving civil servants to conduct its business, even at national level; an arrangement which was FDA practice before 1974. By contrast, the IPCS has a headquarters staff of about 100. The structure of unions like the IPCS, the CPSA and the SCPS is complicated. This is mainly because of the sheer numbers and range of work of members and their interests; the often wide geographical distribution of the membership; and the differing employing bodies dealt with. All the unions are democratic in formal structure with an annual conference, an elected national executive, and a branch organization. This is supplemented in some cases by section and regional organizations, and by special conferences of the kind that the SCPS and the CPSA, for example, held on pay strategy in late 1982. Inevitably, though, union officials and the politically extremist members of national executives exercise disproportionate influence. While Conservative voters are doubtless numerous in the CPSA membership – if not in a natural majority as in the IPCS – the activists in that union, like the CSCA before it, seem well described by its official historian as being engaged in a running war between the moderates and the left. What had changed about the CPSA compared with the old CSCA was that it had become a relatively youthful union. In the 1970s at least, after an average of seven years, the ablest clerical officers were promoted to executive officer and joined the SCPS. The CPSA's historian reflected in 1980 that the membership seemed very different in tone from that of the past: 'the cheering and jeering youngsters at the Conferences of today, some with tangled beards, jeans and tee shirts, seem to have little in common with their bowler-hatted predecessors in striped trousers'.[4]

While the civil service unions have always retained the right to conduct bilateral negotiations with the Treasury (or, when it existed, the CSD) and other departments where appropriate, the main framework of their activity has conventionally been that set by the Whitley system of joint consultation. That system comprises the National Whitley Council (NWC), which deals with matters affecting more than one department, and Departmental Whitley Councils (DWCs) for individual departments. All councils can establish subcommittees, and DWCs can set up committees for local offices and establishments. Whitley bodies are intended to be within reach of all staff and aims are wide, for example 'to secure the greatest measure of co-operation between the administration and the general body of staff'. The councils and committees consist of Official Side and Trade Union Side (until 1980, Staff Side) representatives. The composition of the Trade Union Side representation varies according to the level of the Whitley body. At national level a substantial proportion of the representatives tend to be full-time union officials, while at local level representatives are generally serving civil servants. The Trade Union Side, which is supposed to represent the staff as a whole and not sectional interests, decides the number of seats to be given to the different unions represented on it, but each union makes its own appointments. All nine major unions have normally been represented at NWC level. In the case of local committees, it is possible for the Trade Union Side to consist of only one union. All Whitley bodies have the power to take decisions: but these are made by discussion and not by voting to try to preserve a co-operative atmosphere. There is no national procedure for resolving disagreements, although some departments have arrangements by which differences can be formally registered and referred to other levels of the Whitley machine within the department. There are no formal links between DWCs and the NWC. While DWCs continue to meet at least once a year, the NWC has met only five times since 1945 (in 1949, 1950, 1977, 1979 and 1980). Business is done in subcommittees or informally; informal contacts being important at all levels of Whitleyism. The NWC should comprise twenty-two from both Sides with a chairman from the Official Side, a vice-chairman from the Trade Union Side and secretaries from both Sides. The Official Side usually only exists on paper, and there in early 1983 it consisted of the then heads of the civil service, the other leading permanent secretaries and other Treasury and MPO officials, and a secretary. At that time, the Trade Union Side had not made their nominations, seeming to treat the NWC as having fallen into disuse.[5]

Although, by 1980, even the CSD had described the Whitley procedures as 'cumbersome and slow' and the Official Side thought them outdated, the main drive for change had come from the unions. 'Strike first and negotiate afterwards', Douglas Houghton, a former general secretary of the IRSF, complained of modern trade unionism in 1970, perhaps sensing that militancy was about to displace old-style Whitleyism – 'common sense given constitutional form'. The reckoning would come around 1980, Houghton believed, and so in a way it did. For, while the 1979 strike had been successful, it had also revealed divisions in the unions' leadership and, it was believed, a need for more effective, co-ordinated central machinery. So, from 30 April 1980, the National Staff Side had been wound up and the Council of Civil Service Unions (CCSU) inaugurated the next day. It was from 1 May 1980 also that the Staff Side changed its name to the Trade Union Side throughout the Whitley system. The CCSU is a larger body than the former National Staff Side, consisting of sixty-three members (CPSA 20, SCPS 11, IPCS 11, IRSF 8, CSU 6, POA 3, AGSRO 2, FDA/AIT 2). The CCSU, which meets at least quarterly, is the co-ordinating body of the trade unions representing non-industrial civil servants and those in analogous employment who belong to those unions. Decisions of the CCSU, its committees and subcommittees are normally made on the basis of consensus. Between CCSU meetings, a Major Policy Committee (on which all the unions are represented) usually meets fortnightly to deal with important policy matters; with a Negotiations Subcommittee (consisting of the principal negotiating officers of the CPSA, IPCS and SCPS, plus the senior CCSU secretariat) covering the intervening period. The CCSU's small secretariat is simply the Staff Side's secretariat by another name. The CCSU first met in July 1980, and six months later the old *Whitley Bulletin* formally disappeared, being replaced by the *Bulletin of the Council of Civil Service Unions*. Although the 60-year-old National Staff Side was described in one of the last *Whitley Bulletins* as 'passing gracefully into retirement',[6] and at the normal civil service retirement age, too, in fact it had been rendered redundant by the change from staff relations to more aggressively conducted industrial relations.

3 From Staff Relations to 'Ordinary Industrial Relations'

The many accounts of Whitleyism have conventionally portrayed its development almost as if it was 'The Greatest Story Ever Told'. Almost lovingly, it is recalled that Whitleyism was not originally intended for the civil service. As J. H. Whitley himself said, Whitleyism was designed to secure 'an improvement in the relations between employers and employed' in what he called 'ordinary industrial relations'. In fact, Whitleyism was an example of the type of wishful thinking about industrial relations that surfaces from time to time in British politics, which looks for a permanent general 'solution' to industrial conflict. The main impetus behind Whitleyism was the government's desire to find a means of moderating the wave of industrial militancy which dated from about 1910 and which had already persisted down to 1917 when the Whitley Committee first reported. Whitleyism was never going to make much difference. 'A complete identity of interests between capital and labour cannot thus be effected', the TUC correctly predicted at the time. The strike wave only really ended with the defeat of the General Strike in 1926. Whitleyism only took firm root in smaller industries – and presumably ones where paternalism predominated anyway – the civil service and local government.[7]

From the government's point of view, this was a poor haul. For the government, unlike the 250 staff associations existing at the time, joint consultation in the civil service was not a much-sought-after prize. The big battalions of organized labour were marshalled elsewhere. The government tried and failed to persuade the staff associations to accept a scheme which 'looked like Whitley, smelt like Whitley, almost tasted like Whitley, but it was not Whitley'. The Civil Service National Whitley Council was established in July 1919, and the first Departmental Whitley Councils were formed shortly afterwards. These developments did not initiate a system of harmonious staff relations. 'During the early years of Whitleyism', Sir Albert Day of Staff Side later wrote, 'relations between the two Sides of the National Council were a blend of starch and dynamite. Each viewed the other with some distrust . . . Some meetings of the Council were chilly gatherings of about fifty men and women' brought together to sit 'most of them, mute and idle while more or less formal business was transacted; others were red hot rows.'[8]

There seems to have been plenty of starch present in interwar Whitleyism but little sign of dynamite exploding, even if some union leaders (such as W. J. Brown of the CSCA) had tempers with a short fuse. The Official Side, with the government behind it, could normally expect to win in the interwar era. For a start, despite some rationalization in the number of staff associations, the opposition was very divided. It was more than the aggressive Brown versus the rest, even if it must have seemed like that at times. As Douglas Houghton later remarked, 'the Staff Side had not come together: they had been thrown together'. Moreover, whether within Whitleyism or in bilateral negotiations, the staff associations were considerably handicapped. As their evidence to the Tomlin Commission of 1929–31 showed, mass unemployment outside the secure haven of the civil service made it very difficult for the staff associations to convincingly argue that the pay and conditions of their members needed much improvement. The government's reaction at the time of the Depression was to restrict the scope of state activity and public expenditure with it. Sympathy for this approach was probably not confined to the Official Side. It must have been present, too, in the Staff Side leadership and among the staff association membership. That the prevalence of middle-class mores among the membership ruled out anything resembling industrial action should have reassured the governments of the period despite indications of support for the General Strike from some staff association leaders. The latter behaviour seems to have been enough to ensure that the Trade Disputes and Trade Unions Act of 1927 banned civil service staff associations from affiliation to either the TUC or the Labour Party. After the General Strike, Douglas Houghton recalled, 'the whole Civil Service staff movement had to possess a passport of respectability to get into any Official Side presence'. Houghton said that 'Sir Russell Scott, the

Official Side Chairman during those years, described himself as an inverted Micawber waiting for something to turn down. Constitutional formalities were insisted upon by the Staff Side because that was the only way of commanding attention. The business transacted at a joint Council could have been done over a cup of tea.'[9]

When, then, was the golden age of Whitleyism? Plainly, it was not the interwar era, on which there seems little reason to dispute Houghton's verdict: 'after the first several euphoric years, gains were small and progress slow'. The golden age began with the Second World War. As one veteran recalled: 'the old arrangements for dilatory discussions in committees, with long intervals between meetings, and all the paraphernalia of minutes, drafts, and approvals of minutes, and so on, and formal committee reports by full Councils – all that business couldn't continue under war conditions'. 'In this new and urgent phase of Whitleyism', Houghton wrote, 'constitutional forms mattered far less than the substance of achievement. Impedimenta were swept away for the ever open door.' By 1945, it seems, 'the real working of the Whitley machine' had preponderantly come to be 'a thing that was done between the Staff Side and the Treasury'. The necessary consultation was done on small joint committees or through personal contacts. Doubtless, as Sir Albert Day later said, the 'compulsion of events helped to produce an atmosphere in which sectional sacrifices of interest were readily made'.[10]

Such unity and urgency of purpose was unsurprising in wartime. What ensured that the change was more permanent was the expansion of the civil service in response not only to the demands of the war; but also to the Coalition government's commitments and the legislation both of it and of the Attlee governments, which substantially changed the scope of state responsibilities, as well as attitudes towards public expenditure. The growth of the civil service was substantial: from 163,000 non-industrial civil servants in 1939 to 499,000 in 1945, and never less than 375,000 thereafter. Nor was this latter growth one of temporary staff. The number of permanent officials doubled between 1939 and 1950, and – against the general trend for the civil service – continued to grow throughout the 1950s. The civil service staff associations naturally expanded too. The CSCA, for example, increased its membership from 65,000 to 135,000 between 1938 and 1943, which then provided the base for further but slower expansion.[11] Full employment changed the balance of power between employers and employed; a change symbolized by the repeal of the Trade Disputes and Trade Unions Act in 1946. Full employment also changed the balance of immediate advantage between working in the civil service and employment outside, something for which the staff associations, understandably, sought compensation.

Staff relations in the civil service, however, remained generally amicable down to the 1960s, despite the ritual differences over pay settlements (which led to the appointment of the Priestley Commission) and the calculated tantrums of the Post Office unions. In marked contrast with the interwar era, the Official Side was conciliatory in its dealings with the Staff Side. One of the Official Side's leading figures, Sir John Winnifrith, wrote of Whitleyism in 1953: 'for every act of negotiation there must be ten of consultation. There must be very few acts indeed on the part of management in the Civil Service which they take without such consultation'. Sir John's maxim was 'when in doubt, consult'. Sir William Armstrong, speaking in 1969, went further. His maxim for the Official Side was 'even when in no doubt, consult'. [12]

The golden age of Whitleyism can now be seen to have been over by 1969. From the departure of the combative W. J. Brown in 1942 onwards, the Whitley system had tended to take on the character of a stately minuet. The desire for something a bit more red-blooded was evident in the words and deeds of civil service union leaders such as W. L. Kendall, the general secretary of the CSCA/CPSA 1967–76. Kendall believed that all that fifty years of Whitleyism had produced was 'the illusion of trade union power and influence' in the civil service. Strike action was needed to introduce a 'great gust of reality into the negotiating chamber'. [13] As noted before, the CSCA adopted a strike policy in 1969 and, as will be seen, it was a weapon which was soon to be used, and which was not used alone. Staff relations in the civil service were becoming more like 'ordinary industrial relations'. Whitleyism was in crisis. What had changed?

First, the trade union movement in general had changed – or, rather, changed back – into a militant posture by the late 1960s. The beginning of the end of the period of quiescence had been signified when the eventual succession to the right-wing Arthur Deakin as general secretary of the Transport and General Workers Union (TGWU) went in 1956 to the immoderate Frank Cousins. It was only the beginning of the end, because, when Cousins lost the London bus strike in 1958, Iain Macleod could still joke that the blinds on his office windows at the Ministry of Labour should be kept drawn so that the press could not photograph the general secretary on his knees trying to obtain a settlement. [14] It was governments who were on their knees by 1969 before militant trade unionists like Cousins's own successor at the TGWU, Jack Jones. At least for the union members concerned, this militancy literally seemed to pay off. Indeed, by the winter of 1969–70, in the face of the twin threat of inflation and rising unemployment – a combination deemed impossible by Keynesians – militancy seemed even more attractive as a means of defending living standards. The lesson was unlikely to be lost on the civil service, within which, on the industrial side, the TGWU, for example, had representation.

Secondly, and it seemed in imitation of outside behaviour, the tone of the leadership of some of the civil service unions changed in the direction of a more radical style, of the kind personified by W. L. Kendall. The extent of this change should not be exaggerated. Many civil service union leaders were still moderates and radical leaders were hardly a complete novelty. W. J. Brown at one time had been a left-wing Labour MP, even if he changed his political spots later. L. C. White, Brown's successor as general secretary of the CSCA 1942–55, served on the editorial board of the *Daily Worker*, and in the CSCA he worked with an Executive dominated by Communists and their allies. White was a member of the Labour Party and denied that he was a Communist. Stanley Mayne was another important left-wing personality in the civil service union movement being, successively, a vice-president of the CSCA, a member of the Executive of the FDA (having been promoted direct from the clerical class of the service to the administrative class in 1939) and then general secretary of the IPCS 1948–61. The investigative journalist, Chapman Pincher, who specialized in defence and security matters, later recalled that Mayne became

> a most excellent contact of mine, providing me with lead after lead . . . I was astonished at the range of his information, which covered all manner of secret areas. If there was anything Mayne did not know he could usually find out because he had branch representatives in every station, including places like Harwell and the Aldermaston atomic weapons establishment. Though he was not allowed inside the most secret areas he had automatic entry to the administration departments to visit his members.

Pincher learnt from a former member of the Communist Party that Mayne was not only a card-carrying member, but also took part in various meetings of party subcommittees. In giving evidence to the Radcliffe Committee on Security Procedures in the Public Service of 1961–2, Pincher volunteered the view that it seemed rather pointless keeping Communists out of secret departments when Communists or near-Communists in civil service unions were allowed access, and cited the example of Mayne. The Radcliffe Committee took the point and later said that

> we enquired into the penetration by Communists of the Civil Service staff associations and trade unions and were disturbed at the number of Communists and Communist sympathizers who were holding positions in those bodies either as permanent full time paid officials or as unpaid officers or members of executive committees. We understand that there is no evidence that the Communists have made any exceptional effort to gain control of these unions, but they appear in fact to have achieved a higher degree of penetration here than in almost any other sector of the trade union movement. No evidence has been brought to our knowledge that Communist union officers, whether serving on a paid or unpaid basis, have been detected in any form of espionage. Nevertheless, we regard this presumably deliberate massing of Communist effort in the Civil Service unions as most dangerous to security, however one defines it.

The committee thought that 'the dangers of the present situation are aggravated by the fact that very few people are aware that they exist'. The committee recommended that any government institution engaged in secret work should have the right to deny access to or refuse to negotiate with, known Communist union officials. One head to roll as the result of the implementation of this recommendation was that of Richard Nunn, Mayne's successor as general secretary of the IPCS. While denying that he was, or ever had been, a member of the Communist Party, Nunn felt obliged to resign in late 1962. Heads also rolled in the CSCA union hierarchy and promotions were blocked. The CSCA's National Executive was almost entirely composed of political moderates by 1966. As the union's official historian said, the old left wave had subsided, but there were signs that a new one was beginning to swell. There were indeed, and not just in the CSCA and its successor union. In 1980 *The Economist* could, without rebuttal, describe the SCPS union leadership as 'Marxist dominated', and this seemed to have been the case for some time. It is difficult to know more than twenty years later whether or not – to repeat the Radcliffe Committee's phrases – 'Communist representation among Civil Service union officials' remained as 'disproportionately high' as it had been in the early 1960s. The Diplock Commission's findings, as made public in 1982, did not deal directly with the matter. The commission believed that 'the threat offered by the Communist Party of Great

Britain (CPGB), upon which Radcliffe concentrated has probably diminished'. The commission cited the fall in CPGB membership, but recognized that this has been 'accompanied by the proliferation of new subversive groups of the extreme Left and extreme Right (mainly the former) whose aim is to overthrow democratic parliamentary government in this country by violent or other unconstitutional means'. Certainly, Marxists are prominent in some civil service union leaderships. If there has been a change, there may be little comfort to be derived from it. The Radcliffe Committee used the terms Communist and Fascist as if they were interchangeable,[15] which was politically unsophisticated, but both Communists and Fascists have in common their desire to undermine liberal democracy. There now seem to be as many different types of socialist as there are of Christian. That a union official or activist is a Marxist but not a member of the CPGB is not necessarily to the advantage of the defenders of the 'open society', not least because the individuals concerned may have wished to avoid the opprobrium that commonly attaches to such membership. The Marxist may not have joined the CPGB or have left it simply out of conviction, but because that person cannot accept its discipline. One act of discipline would be to require a sympathizer to work for the party outside CPGB ranks. The Marxist remains committed to victory in the class struggle, and the aim of this is to undermine the state.

What, above all, sent Whitleyism into crisis, and provided union leaderships, Marxist or not, with an incentive, where one was needed to be combative, was the marked change in the direction of militancy of the rank and file of the civil service unions. Again, this change should not be exaggerated. After all, the historian of the CPSA began his book with a chapter called 'On the combative character of civil service clerks' and demonstrated there that this aggressiveness was nothing new. To some extent this may be a consequence of knowledge of popular dislike of civil servants. As one former civil servant remarked:

> . . .it would not be surprising if the average civil servant was influenced by the doubts cast upon the necessity for what he is doing, or if his pride in the Service or in his own department was shaken by the popular estimate of their efficiency. In a money-conscious, status-seeking society it is natural that he should think of this month's pay, next year's promotion and the eventual pension; and if circumstances make it hard for him to be motivated by more exalted considerations he is quite likely to become obsessed by these tangible ones.

Before 1956, when the Priestley 'fair comparisons' pay formula was agreed, the main tangible attractions of the civil service were security of tenure and generous pension and annual leave arrangements. The pay could be seen as modest, but at least it was assured and there were identifiable incremental scales. What Priestley offered in an expansive era, and substantially without loss of existing benefits, was the prospect of real money in the form of pay comparable with that in the flourishing parts of the private sector. Scarcely had this prize been secured when the Pay Pause of 1961–2 became the first of the incomes policies which threatened to take it away. The accelerating inflation that caused these policies, and which was not for long arrested by them, was a threat, too, in persistently devaluing gains and in requiring updating settlements. Before Priestley was implemented, the civil service unions and their members were striving for their taste of honey: after that, their militancy was largely directed towards keeping it. An early indication of what lay ahead came in 1962 when, at the time of the Pay Pause, G. F. Green, a moderate, seemed to be leading the CSCA to defeat in salary negotiations, the membership's representatives ensured his removal from the general secretaryship.[16] What followed was the eventual emergence of a more aggressive union leadership, and one more and more likely to attract support from memberships which proved to be no longer so inhibited by traditional middle-class mores about strike action.

The first civil service strike followed in 1973, taking the form of a one-day stoppage involving the CPSA, the Society of Civil Servants and the Customs and Excise Group on 27 February. 'However good our system and however well based our institutions', Leslie Williams of the National Staff Side wrote of Whitleyism a year later, 'they cannot . . . go on surviving the kind of continuous attack that we have had over the last ten years.' He pointed to the divisions on the Staff Side, and between the Staff Side and union members some of whom saw it as a 'buffer' between them and 'the enemy'. Williams recognized that while the 'cordial and sound relationship' enjoyed with the Official Side of the NWC was valuable, it was 'not a substitute for winning the support of the rank and file members' of the unions. In fact, as the Staff Side's journal later remarked, 'troubles of 1973' meant that 'Civil Service industrial relations' had 'altered direction dramatically and the old world of Whitleyism' had 'changed profoundly'.[17]

Where did Whitleyism and the civil service union movement go now? The Staff Side's solution advanced in 1974 was naturally to strengthen the central machinery. The discussion document concerned pointed out that the National Staff Side office, consisting as it does of only three negotiating officers, the Secretary General, the Secretary and the Assistant Secretary, assisted by a Research Officer and a small team of supporting office staff, has been expected over the years to carry out its negotiating role on behalf of constituent organizations and their memberships with very limited resources.

The Staff Side recognized that the achievement of an objective such as 'closer co-ordination in dealing with all aspects of pay policy' meant 'the development of more comprehensive concepts of democracy and accountability' involving the mass membership than currently existed. The Staff Side envisaged three possible developments. The first was the creation of a single civil service trade union. The second was a closer degree of federation than that which was represented by the National Staff Side and its existing machinery. The third was for arrangements to continue much as they were. As the discussion document recognized, 'the concept of a single trade union could well be regarded as demanding too radical a departure from the long established traditions of the Civil Service trade union movement to be contemplated, particularly as a direct transition from the existing system'.[18] So it proved. Ideas about federation rather than unification were also seen as too radical.

The civil service union movement was, nevertheless, still changing in the 1970s at a pace which was swift by past standards. There were several important union mergers. In 1973, for example, the CPSA absorbed the Ministry of Labour Staff Association and in 1974 the County Court Officers Association was amalgamated with it too. At the beginning of 1975 the Customs and Excise Group and the Association of Officers of the Ministry of Labour merged with the SCS. It might have been expected that the contemporary fashion for creating large ministries and for 'hiving off' functions, combined with structural changes in the civil service following the Fulton Report, would promote an atmosphere conducive to union mergers. To some extent, as we have seen, this occurred. However, while, for instance, the creation of the administration group had removed many of the formal working barriers between the memberships concerned, such close links as were established between the FDA and the SCS were soon severed, and a proposed merger between the SCS and the CPSA came to nothing in 1976. The then moderately led SCS had its own problems with what it considered poaching on its territory by the Association of Scientific, Technical and Mangerial Staffs (ASTMS); a threat to which a former general secretary attributed by SCS's demonstration of virility in participating in the 1973 stoppage. The SCS ended the threat from ASTMS by affiliating to the TUC in 1973, and thus securing the protection of the Bridlington Agreement. The SCS membership had been previously opposed to links with the TUC, having reaffirmed this position as recently as 1970. The IPCS joined the TUC in 1976, similarly overcoming traditional reluctance; and when in 1977 the FDA and the AIT followed suit this meant that all the Staff Side's constituent unions had taken this step.[19] The main motive behind this burst of affiliating activity was probably the feeling that there were now material losses in remaining outside the TUC.

Material gain was the motive behind a further outburst of industrial action in the civil service towards the end of the Winter of Discontent of 1978–9. After the manner in which the Callaghan government had handled the 1978 pay settlement, the Staff Side had talked of 'the Big One coming up in 1979'. From 23 February 1979 onwards, the CPSA and the SCPS conducted a campaign of one-day and selective strikes in support of pay claims, and inflicted a severe defeat on the Labour government. 'After nine weeks of industrial action the government was ready to settle on a pay rise worth more than three times their original cash limits. Instead of their 5% norm, we won a settlement worth 16.5%', the SCPS journal, *Opinion*, recalled two years later.

The Press enjoyed mocking the idea of civil servants on strike . . . Within a few days, however, the action was being taken rather more seriously. Drug companies, car exporters, farmers and defence contractors were furious at not getting hundreds of thousands of pounds due to them. Deputations of City businessmen arrived at Society Headquarters asking for the strike at Companies House to be called off. Freight transport firms, hit by Customs strikes, suddenly began urging Government to pay civil servants a fair salary. The Department of National Savings took out advertisements apologizing for services to savers being halted. Emergency legislation was rushed through Parliament to try and cope with the total closure of courts in Scotland. NATO exercises were disrupted by action in MOD. The Government's financial operations were severely disrupted for months . . . As VAT payments were halted by action at Southend, Government borrowing soared. Balance of payments figures could not be published, and for months the Treasury's figures on the crucial Public Sector Borrowing Requirement were distorted by the effects of action. The very core of Government economic policy was shaken: in November 1979, Sir Geoffrey Howe increased Minimum Lending Rate by a record 3%, and explained that this was largely due to the effects of the Civil Service strike and the later Post Office strike which also involved Society and CPSA members.[20]

However successful in its outcome, as we have noted, the 1979 strike led to differences within the National Staff Side and, after a review of its organization conducted under the aegis of the secretary-general, W. L. Kendall, that body was replaced by the CCSU in May 1980, and the Staff Side was translated into the Trade Union Side throughout the Whitley machinery. There seemed little point in the reconstruction which had led to the establishment of the CCSU if there was not to be more central direction of the unions and their membership. A very loose confederation had been changed into a much more integrated organization which could be expected, at least for a time, to act more like a federation. Plainly, the intention was to confront the Conservative government. In March 1980 the unions were clear that they were 'busily engaged in making contingency plans just in case the Government is ill advised enough to interfere with the outcome of this year's pay review'. Having inherited the consequences of the 1979 strike, and having experienced, too, the unprecedented IPCS strike of that summer – which, among other things, interfered with the running of the armed forces – the Thatcher government could have had no illusions about the civil service unions' response when, in October 1980, it unilaterally ended the Priestley pay research system and combined this with a denial of access to the PRU's findings and to arbitration. A Cabinet committee of civil servants known as EOCS (Economy Official Civil Service), meeting in the Old Admiralty Building, drew up the government's contingency plans to meet the inevitable strike. From what the unions called their communications centre in Rochester Row, the CCSU secretary P. D. Jones saw things in military terms: 'we are just like rival headquarters. We have had the Phoney War. Our Dunkirk was the suspension of pay research and we are now approaching our Finest Hour. There will be a D-Day.'[21]

While expressions of this kind were in accord with the exaggerated style of civil service union leadership pioneered by W. J. Brown, those outside that tradition could suggest that using D-Day as an analogy with civil service industrial action was inappropriate. Among the reasons that D-Day was successful was that the Germans wrongly believed that the Allied invasion would come in the Pas de Calais rather than Normandy, a misjudgement which adversely affected the disposition of their resources. After its predecessor's experiences in 1979, the Thatcher government knew where the civil service unions would strike in 1981, and knew also that – unlike the Allies in 1944 – the unions were equipped only for a guerrilla campaign and not a substantial all-out assault. Further, the Germans in 1944 were heavily engaged elsewhere, principally on the Eastern Front. For the Thatcher government, the battle against inflation was treated as its overwhelming priority – its Eastern Front. From its perspective, the striking civil servants seemed to be willing to act as shock troops for the other side. If military analogies had to be used, for the civil service unions it was not D-Day but Stalingrad which was in prospect: but with Mrs Thatcher cast as the triumphant Marshal Zhukov, and with W. L. Kendall playing the role of General von Paulus, forced to surrender after a long and costly campaign.

Provided the government acted as if it would prefer to fall rather than to concede, which seemed to be the attitude of the Prime Minister and the Treasury ministers from the outset, if not that of Lord Soames and Barney Hayhoe at the CSD, then the civil service strike of 1981 was bound to result in a CCSU defeat. During the weeks before the strike, to avert other industrial action, the government had felt the need to make substantial concessions to the miners and the water workers. There was no possibility of comparable dislocation or risk of defeat in the prospective civil service strike. Although, for the first time, all nine unions in the CCSU were involved, including the FDA, the worst that the civil servants could do was to re-run 1979 all over again, if at greater length, and the consequences of this were deemed bearable by the government. So, when the CCSU declined to accept the government's 7 per cent offer and pressed its 15 per cent pay claim by means of industrial action doomed to failure, its perverse achievement was to provide the Thatcher government with the victory that it badly needed to lend credence to its counter-inflation strategy. The CCSU picked the wrong opponent – Margaret Thatcher – and the wrong time to fight. 'To hell with it . . . our side it not prepared to play games any longer', W. L. Kendall pronounced as pay negotiations failed.[22] But this time the 'game', unlike that in 1979, was not being 'played' against a dispirited minority Labour government, facing likely election defeat and well aware that the public sector salatariat was one of its few growing areas of support. The Conservative government's situation and interests were different. It had a good majority and possibly three more years before an election. It had a Prime Minister who, despite the pressure of 'world opinion', showed contemporaneously that she was prepared to let IRA hunger strikers die in Northern Ireland's Maze prison rather than grant them political status. In fact, Mrs Thatcher was not 'playing games' at all.

The civil service strike of 1981 began on 9 March, the day before the budget, with a twenty-four-hour stoppage intended to be total. The CCSU felt able to claim that 450,000 or 85 per cent of civil servants had observed the stoppage. The CSD's calculation was 275,000 or 52 per cent. The strike then lasted for twenty-one weeks. Aside from a further one-day stoppage on 1 April and a half-day stoppage on 14 April, both less well observed than that of 9 March, the strike was prosecuted by selective action. 'We have concentrated our main effort on hitting the government machine', the CCSU stated, 'Adverse effects upon the general public have been minimized to a considerable extent.' So, computers were the obvious targets: notably the VAT computer at Southend, the Paymaster-General's computer at Crawley, the DHSS computer at Newcastle and the PAYE computer at Shipley. As in 1979 the operations of Companies House were disrupted and so was the Scottish legal system. As in 1979, too, NATO exercises were interfered with. There were strikes at intelligence monitoring stations. In mid-April disruption to the servicing of Britain's nuclear submarines at Faslane was such that a senior union official suggested that when one of them, *HMS Resolution,* eventually set sail she would be 'a cardboard cut-out submarine' because the Royal Navy was not able to rearm her. The MOD denied this. On 21 May the CCSU claimed that three of Britain's four Polaris submarines were 'trapped' as a result of selective strikes in Scotland. When asked about the danger to Britain's nuclear deterrent, W. L. Kendall replied: 'I'll be on the end of a phone if anybody wants to ring me up about some great invasion.'[23]

The CCSU strategy emphasized the disruption of defence establishments, revenue collection and the gathering of statistics. This was widely said to be a sophisticated strategy and it certainly seemed well planned. Nevertheless, there were also obvious reasons why it was the only one available to the CCSU: namely, the likely lack of support for more sustained, extensive, incisive action from either the public, the TUC, or, it was feared, probably most union members. At a time of rising unemployment, outside sympathy for civil servants, with job security, striking for what many might well see as still better pay and conditions was almost bound to be minimal. The CCSU strikes did interfere with the issue of passports, for example, and, for a time, they did disrupt airports (despite the fact that the Civil Aviation Authority was not a party to the dispute, and its employees were not civil servants). Generally, though, the CCSU's approach was aimed at not antagonizing the public, which would certainly have occurred if the unions had gone beyond halting computer operations and had halted social security payments. The TUC, moreover, had ruled out action which would hurt the old, the sick and the unemployed and, where appropriate, emergency benefit procedure ensured that the payments were made. In return for this restraint, all the TUC leadership did was to express general support, and make gestures such as declining to cross a picket line to go to an NEDC meeting and referring the dispute to the International Labour Organization. [24]

So when W. L. Kendall said that the CCSU was going to 'put the boot in' with its programme of selective strikes, that was exactly what the unions did not dare to do. Moreover, even if they had taken the risk, some of them perhaps had good cause to doubt the resolve of their memberships. Predictions of the kind made by Tony Christopher (IRSF) that 'the whole Civil Service will revolt against its employer' always seemed optimistic. After three months it was evident that the unions were in financial difficulties in sustaining the 5,000 or so selective strikers because their members had not paid the strike levy in sufficient numbers. Having scorned earlier, and unnecessary, promises from the government about the following year's pay claim not being constrained by cash limits and a guarantee of access to arbitration then, the CCSU could not expect a positive response when, in late May, it dropped its 15 per cent claim. A 'significant gesture' said the IPCS's William McCall. Indeed it was, for it signified eventual surrender. 'We have a Government which believes that it can beat down the Civil Service and make us crawl back to work', the SCPS's B. A. Gillman complained. What he said may have been melodramatic, but Mr Gillman rightly seemed to sense that the government wished to inflict a major defeat on the CCSU. 'The Government has the Civil Service unions in an armlock', *The Economist* observed in early June, and it seemed in no hurry to release it. The appointment of the Megaw Committee in late June merely emphasized that pay research would not be restored. At last, on 16 July, the government presented the CCSU with an opportunity for submission when it marginally improved its original offer (costing £230 million in a full year) with a £30 a head offer (costing £15 million). Though this offer was well short of the CCSU's original claim (which would have cost £550 million), the unions felt forced to accept it. The membership of all the unions except that of the IRSF (by a narrow majority) declined to pursue the only real alternative, an indefinite all-out strike. In this manner, the civil service strike of 1981 ended on 30 July. Although soon surpassed by the NHS strike of 1982, it was at the time the longest national industrial dispute since the miners' stoppages which followed the General Strike of 1926. [25]

As a result of the CCSU's 'first foray into the field of direct action', its secretary, P. D. Jones believed, 'the Civil Service trade union movement has come of age'. He added: 'those who write off our action as a failure should reserve judgment. The long term benefits may well even prove the general media view that neither side won, nor lost, as being wrong, and that the industrial action was not only inevitable, but successful too'. There was, of course, the possibility that, as the Heath government had done after defeating the postal strike of 1971, the Thatcher government would throw away its victory. There was also the possibility that, in 1982, the Civil Service Arbitration Tribunal would throw away the victory for it and, in fact, the gains were modified. Nevertheless, whatever the media said, the immediate result of the civil service strike of 1981 was a government victory. As Mr Kendall conceded, the CCSU had been forced to accept a 'thoroughly unsatisfactorily pay settlement'.[26]

What the formation of the CCSU, with its arrangements for co-ordinated action, and then the 1981 strike, had emphasized was the importance of the question of the constitutionality of aggressive civil service unionism. P. D. Jones had perceptively recognized the problem several months before the suspension of pay research, predicting that 'a major confrontation posing a major constitutional crisis is not too far away'. He saw the elected government as an 'immovable object' and civil service union militancy as an 'irresistible force'. Ministers now had to judge whether their staff would implement their measures. In some circumstances, Jones envisaged the government being rendered 'virtually powerless'. He believed that 'consideration needs to be given to the constitutional implications of increasing militancy in the Civil Service unions'. A more common view, however, seemed to be that expressed by the SCPS's B. A. Gillman as the 1981 strike loomed:

> when employers try to curb wages and cut their jobs their workers and their unions usually oppose them − naturally. Yet this unremarkable fact gives rise to heated indignation in some quarters when the employer is the Government and the unions are Civil Service unions. Union opposition is criticized as being 'political' and thus illegitimate. It is indeed political, because government policies make it so, but it is not only legitimate, but vital for a modern democracy, that this opposition should be mounted.[27]

When the CCSU's declared ambition in the 1981 strike was 'to blow the Government's economic strategy right off course', then there plainly *is* a constitutional issue involved in militant civil service unionism. If the British Constitution is based on any theory it is that government action is legitimized by electoral processes, and that a special legitimacy attaches to action which has been proposed by a party victorious at a general election. At the same time, civil servants are legally and morally entitled to organize for their own benefit. When both aims cannot be achieved, the outcome of the conflict should be that the government is successful. So, constitutionally, the kind of 'opposition' which Mr Gillman favoured is bound to be illegitimate. The notion, which he developed, that civil servants have some kind of special licence, based on working knowledge, to criticize the effects of public expenditure cuts and cash limits is the very opposite of the constitutional position. The Thatcher government was elected on a programme involving such cuts and limits. They were, and remained, at the core of the economic strategy which the unions hoped to overturn. Whether or not, as Mr Gillman alleged, the Conservative government had exhibited 'a naked political bias',[28] it was a bias which had been displayed before, and approved by a sufficient number of the electorate. Moreover, it was an electorate which did not accord the civil service unions some right of veto to be used against governments which declined to maintain the previous scale of state activity and particular numbers of expectations of civil servants. Indeed, the civil service is organized on the principle that it is a non-political instrument for implementing government policy and to the extent that union activity conflicted with that principle it is unconstitutional.

Clearly, only old-style Whitleyism can be readily reconcilable with a non-political civil service. The politicization of the unions seems to have gone too far for this to easily occur. Partly, but not mainly, this is a matter of Marxist penetration. Mrs Kate Losinska, when CPSA president in 1976, depicted Marxists in her union as 'following a blueprint that helped bring control in Eastern Europe'. Mrs Losinska found subsequent campaigning in the moderate cause hazardous. On 26 October 1978 she was pushed down the stairs at a union meeting in Glasgow. She broke her leg. Her assailant escaped. Mrs Losinska persisted to secure the presidency again, her successor in 1982 being a member of the Militant Tendency. His election may have been assisted by a low poll, and one notes that as recently as 1980 the CPSA membership rejected a move to affiliate it to the Labour Party. Nevertheless, although an admirer of the Prime Minister, Mrs Losinska felt the need to picket Downing Street at the outset of the 1981 strike. Plainly union responsibilities dictated such behaviour. 'I would lose my job if I accepted the offer we have been made today', K. R.

Thomas, the CPSA's general secretary, had said earlier. He was probably right. The Priestley honey pot was too tasty for the rank-and-file activists to give up without a fight. Its removal from time to time had merely served to whet the appetite. The prospect of permanent denial seemed to be too much to bear, at least for some. Where the process of withdrawal will lead to in the civil service union movement was difficult to judge in the immediate aftermath of the 1981 strike because the evidence available was conflictual. Centripetal tendencies remained TUC membership and links with other public sector unions, and the CCSU machinery. The prospective IPCS–ASGRO merger and the revived proposal for an SCPS–CPSA merger suggested further concentration. That centrifugal tendencies also exist is evident from the formation – as a break-away from the left-wing-controlled SCPS – of an Immigration Service Union in the Home Office, recognized for departmental purposes in 1982; and by the advent of the Ministry of Defence Staff Association, also anti-Marxist, and committed to an anti-strike policy. The local co-ordinating committees dating from the 1981 strike – which remain in existence outside the normal union machinery and are not obviously under effective central control – would also seem to be a centrifugal force. In establishing these committees, one union leader recognized at the time, 'we may have created our own Frankenstein's Monster'. Whether the government is capable of slaughtering this 'Monster' largely depends on displaying the same determination shown in breaking, in January 1983, the five-month SCPS/CPSA strike in DHSS offices in Oxford and Birmingham. Other union members were insufficiently supportive, and indeed some were among the 800 officials who manned emergency payment centres and, thus, broke the strike.[29] While the largest civil service unions have difficulties with activists, contrary to leadership rhetoric their memberships are hardly in the same league as that of the National Union of Mineworkers of the 1970s when it comes to effective militancy. Nevertheless, the civil service unions have shown themselves capable of effective obstructionism and, thus confronted by their own direct employees, governments may well not forever rule out measures designed to politically neutralize those unions.

References

1 *Whitley Bulletin,* December 1979, p. 165; E. Wigham, *From Humble Petition to Militant Action. A History of the Civil and Public Services Association 1903–1978* (London, 1980), pp. 151–2; *The Economist,* 26 July 1975, pp. 25–6.

2 CSD, *The Civil Service: Introductory Factual Memorandum Submitted to the House of Commons Treasury and Civil Service Committee* (1980), p. 28; *Whitley Bulletin,* January 1980, p. 11.

3 *CCSU Bulletin,* January/February 1982, pp. 54–63.

4 FDA, *Introducing the FDA,* n.d., and information 25 July 1980; AGSRO, *Constitution and Rules* (1979 edn) and information 3 December 1980; information from AIT 22 May 1981; CPSA, *Rules*

and Constitution, September 1980; CSU, *Rules* (1979 edn) and information 21 January 1981; *IRSF Members Handbook and Diary for 1981,* pp. 6–17; IPCS information 23 September 1980; POA, *Rules and Constitution* (1979 edn) and information 14 April 1981; *SCPS Diary 1981,* p. 4; P. Drake *et al., Which Way Forward. An Interim Review of Issues for the SCPS,* September 1980; *Opinion,* August 1982, pp. 6–7; Wigham, *Humble Petition,* pp. 9–10.

5   CSD, *Introductory Factual Memorandum,* pp. 29–30, 35; H. Parris, *Staff Relations in the Civil Service. Fifty Years of Whitleyism* (London, 1973), p. 63; *Whitley Bulletin,* September/October 1980, pp. 134–6; information from MPO (11 February 1983), CCSU (25 January 1983).

6   CSD, *Introductory Factual Memorandum,* p. 32; D. Houghton, 'Foreword' in J. D. Thomas, *Fifty Years of Whitleyism in the Inland Revenue 1920–1970* (London, 1970), p. 5; *Whitley Bulletin,* May 1979, pp. 67–8, and March 1980, p. 34, and June 1980, p. 89; *CCSU Bulletin,* February 1981, pp. 29–31. P. D. Jones, 'The council of civil service unions', *Management Services in Government,* vol. 35 (1980), pp. 136–40.

7   L. D. White, *Whitley Councils in the British Civil Service. A Study in Conciliation and Arbitration* (Chicago, 1933), pp. 4–5; K. Middlemas, *Politics in Industrial Society. The Experience of the British System since 1911* (London, 1979), pp. 137–8.

8   F. Stack, 'Civil service associations and the Whitley Report of 1917', *Political Quarterly,* vol. 40 (1969), pp. 283–95; G. H. Stuart-Bunning, 'The birth of Whitley', *Whitley Bulletin,* May 1946, pp. 27–8; A. J. T. Day, 'Negotiation and joint consultation in the civil service', *Whitley Bulletin,* July 1953, p. 102.

9   B. V. Humphreys, *Clerical Unions in the Civil Service* (Oxford, 1958), pp. 176–81; D. Houghton, 'Whitley jubilee. The first twenty years 1920–40', *Whitley Bulletin,* June 1969, pp. 85, 89.

10   ibid, pp. 88–9; Parris, *Staff Relations,* pp. 59–62.

11   *Civil Service Statistics 1971* (1971), p. 14; Wigham, *Humble Petition,* p. 218.

12   Sir J. Winnifrith, 'Negotiation and joint consultation in the civil service', *Whitley Bulletin,* July 1953, p. 105; Sir W. Armstrong, 'Whitleyism in the civil service', *Whitley Bulletin,* November 1969, p. 154.

13   *Red Tape,* December 1969, pp. 69–70.

14   N. Fisher, *Iain Macleod* (London, 1973), pp. 129–30.

15   Wigham, *Humble Petition,* pp. 45–50, 80–1, 89–90, 94, 113–21; J. E. Mortimer and V. A. Ellis, *A Professional Union. The Evolution of the Institution of Professional Civil Servants* (London, 1980), pp. 128–9, 152–3, 214, 222–3, 235–7, 245, 300, 399–400; C. Pincher, *Inside Story. A Documentary of the Pursuit of Power* (London, 1979 edn), pp. 332–3; *Security Procedures in the Public Service,* Cmnd 1681 (1962), pp. 3, 9; *The Economist,* 17 May 1980, p. 50; *Statement on the Recommendations of the Security Commission* (Diplock Report), Cmnd 8540 (1982), pp. 3–4.

16   Wigham, *Humble Petition,* pp. 8–11, 138–40; N. Walker, *Morale in the Civil Service. A Study of the Desk Worker* (Oxford, 1961), p. 254.

17   Sir L. Williams, 'Industrial relations in the civil service', *Management Services in Government,* vol. 29 (1974), pp. 180–1; *Whitley Bulletin,* March 1973, pp. 33, 37 and March 1979, p. 33.

18   Civil Service National Whitley Council (Staff Side), *Future of the Civil Service Trade Union Movement* (1974), pp. 7–13.

19   Wigham, *Humble Petition,* pp. 170–2; Williams, 'Industrial relations', pp. 178, 182; *Civil Service Opinion,* July 1973, pp. 212–14, and September 1974, p. 231, and December 1974, p. 323; Mortimer and Ellis, *Professional Union,* pp. 140–2, 217, 230–2, 294–7, 358–9, 371–4, 424; *Whitley Bulletin,* June 1973, p. 81, and August 1977, p. 113.

20   *Whitley Bulletin,* June 1978, p. 90; *Opinion,* February 1981, p. 4.

21   *Whitley Bulletin,* May 1979, pp. 67–8, and March 1980, p. 33; *State Service,* November 1979, pp. 334–5, and December 1979, pp. 362–4, and January 1980, pp. 4, 10 and February 1980, pp. 54–5; *The Times,* 25 November 1980.

22   *The Times,* 4 March 1981.

23   *The Economist,* 14 March 1981, p. 26, 18 April 1981, p. 21 and 16 May 1981, p. 43; *CCSU Campaign Report,* no. 1, March 1981, p. 2, and no. 2, 23 April 1981, pp. 1, 4, and no. 6, 21 May 1981, p. 2; *Financial Times,* 2 April 1981; *The Times,* 27 May 1981; *CCSU Bulletin,* September/October 1981, p. 126.

24   *The Times,* 12 May 1981; *CCSU Bulletin,* March 1982, p. 65.

25 *The Times*, 10 March 1981, 23 April 1981; *CCSU Campaign Report*, no. 9, 11 June 1981, p. 1; *Opinion*, August 1981, pp. 1, 3; *Financial Times*, 22 June 1981, 17 July 1981, 21 July 1981, 22 July 1981, 30 July 1981; *Guardian*, 27 May 1981, 8 June 1981, 31 July 1981.

26 *CCSU Bulletin*, September/October 1981, pp. 121–2.

27 *The Times*, 9 May 1950, *The Economist*, 17 May 1980, p. 9; *Opinion*, February 1981, p. 2.

28 *Guardian*, 9 March 1981 (W. L. Kendall); *Opinion*, February 1981, p. 2.

29 K. Losinska, 'The Marxist battle for Britain: central and local government', *Reader's Digest*, February 1976, p. 59; *The Economist*, 2 December 1978, p. 24 and 22 May 1982, p. 34; *Red Tape*, July/August 1980, pp. 317–18 and January 1983, p. 4; *Opinion*, February 1983, pp. 1, 8; *IPCS Bulletin*, 6 December 1982, p. 1; *The Times*, 24 February 1981; *Financial Times*, 30 March 1981; *Sunday Telegraph*, 6 June 1982; *Guardian*, 2 October 1982, 7 October 1982, 13 December 1982, 17 December 1982, 6 January 1983, 8 January 1983.

7 The Quest for an 'Efficient' Civil Service

If the Fulton Committee's strategy was 'to toss a number of high explosive bombs' at the home civil service in order to justify a programme of 'radical change' — as its secretary, R. W. L. Wilding said that it was — the service could reasonably expect that what was effectively a Fabian group — and, hence, believers in bureaucratic social engineering — would aim to leave the essential framework in place. 'Though not without recommendations for change', Sir James Dunnett, one of the committee later said, the Fulton Report was 'broadly conservative'. This combination of conservatism and radicalism came out in Fulton's recommendations relating to the structure of the home civil service. 'The problems of structure would in some ways be much simpler if each department employed its own staff independently, and constructed its own grading system to fit the precise needs of its own work and staff', the committee wrote, 'But the Civil Service cannot be run in this way . . . the Service must be a flexible, integrated whole; it must continue to be a unified Service. Its structure should be designed accordingly as a structure that is common throughout.' Sir Warren Fisher might have said much the same. Given that, although unknowingly, Fulton was reacting against the Fisher inheritance, it was strange that the committee ruled out re-creating a structure which, allowing for the subsequent growth of the service, would resemble the pre-1914 departmentalized structure that Fisher had deplored and which would cramp the style of 'the generalist' against whom Fulton had directed so much of its fire. A unified grading structure covering the service from top to bottom seems to have been recommended by Fulton in imitation of British Petroleum: but its implementation would also have the effect of taking Fisher's logic to its extremes — the universalization throughout the service of a structure ('essentially a pay structure') paid scant regard to the range and complexity of work done by half a million civil servants, and did not readily relate to Fulton's proposals that 'business methods' such as 'accountable management' should be introduced into the service. It was, after all, to remain a career service and one in which staff costs, the predominant element in departmental running costs, were to remain broadly standardized and not necessarily related to performance. While some of Fulton's 'radical' ideas were taken up, for fifteen years unified grading made little progress.[1]

The Thatcher government had an advantage over the Fulton Committee in that its commitment to 'business methods' cohered more readily with its philosophy. It attained office determined to 'de-privilege' the civil service and pledged to cut its overall size. There seems little doubt that there was scope for such a 'rationalization' of the home civil service in 1979, as Table 7.1 demonstrates. The growth in the size of the administration group was remarkable in the 1970s, and the expansion that took place, for instance at senior principal, principal, SEO, HEO and EO levels was suggestive of 'grade drift' in the face of successive incomes policies and of slack standards of staff inspection. The Conservative government was better placed than its predecessors to secure reduced numbers because unlike them it was prepared to envisage reduced functions. Unlike with Fulton, the civil servants could not be so sure this time that their hierarchies and privileges would emerge unscathed. That some of the Thatcher government's 'bombs' did not land properly (such as those directed against index-linked pensions) did not slow down the onslaught. The civil service's pay system was destroyed. The service's unions were defeated in the 1981 strike, and this victory was consolidated with the abolition of the CSD and the return of central responsibility for the service's pay and conditions to the Treasury. The casualties included two permanent secretaries, one of them, Sir Ian Bancroft, the head of the home civil service. It would be difficult to think of an action better designed to remind the remaining permanent secretaries and the mass of civil servants below them of their own vulnerability and of the supremacy of ministers. As the Thatcher government pursued its manpower targets allied to cash limits on expenditure, the civil service was being chopped back in a sustained manner for the first time in normal peacetime conditions. The Wardale inquiry into staffing at 'open structure' level and the Rayner scrutinies were part of this drive for a smaller, more 'efficient' civil service, which the Conservative government eventually sought to translate into something resembling a long-term strategy.

The example that was followed was that set by Michael Heseltine when he was Secretary of State for the Environment. Knowledge of private sector management practice, together with his experience as Minister for Aerospace, led Heseltine, on coming to the DoE in 1979, to introduce there a Management Information System for Ministers

Table 7.1   *The Effect of the Thatcher Government's Cuts on Civil Service Numbers*

Grades/Groups	1.4.70	1.4.79	1.4.82	% Increase 1970–9	% Cut 1979–82
Non-Industrial Civil Service	493,000	565,815	527,970	14·8	6·7
Open Structure	664	823	743	23·9	9·7
Administrative Group	243,879	299,882	284,155	23·0	5·2
Assistant secretary	1,048	1,245	1,084	18·8	12·9
Senior principal	502	812	694	61·8	14·5
Principal	3,195	4,608	4,146	40·2	10·0
Senior executive officer	5,789	8,489	7,676	46·6	9·5
Higher executive officer	16,866	25,198	23,941	49·4	5·0
Executive officer (inc local officer 1)	46,305	62,479	61,538	34·9	1·5
Clerical officer/clerical assistant (inc local officer 2)	170,174	197,051	185,076	15·8	6·1
Science Group and Related Grades	17,970	17,284	15,784	–3·8	8·7
Deputy chief scientific officer	177	205	191	15·8	6·8
Senior principle scientific officer	579	716	706	23·7	1·4
Principal scientific officer	1,898	2,477	2,303	30·5	7·0
Senior scientific officer	3,485	3,734	3,421	7·1	8·4
Higher scientific officer	4,179	4,072	3,750	–2·6	7·9
Scientific officer/asst scientific officer	7,652	6,080	5,413	–20·5	11·0
Professional and Technology Group and Related Grades	40,235	41,114	36,728	2·2	10·7
Director B (introduced 1.4.72)	—	164	143	—	12·8
Superintending Grades	485	676	628	39·4	7·1
Principal P and T officer	1,956	2,515	2,359	28·6	6·2
P and T officer I	4,818	5,865	5,483	21·7	8·5
P and T officer II	7,688	8,690	7,967	13·0	8·3
P and T officer III	11,533	11,836	10,477	2·6	11·5
P and T officer IV	13,755	11,368	9,671	–17·4	14·9

Source: IPCS Bulletin, 8/83, p. 9.

(MINIS) which would enable him to be aware of 'who does what, why and what does it cost?' in that department. His need for such information was understandable, given that – in 1981, for instance – he had to deal with no fewer than forty-eight under secretaries. In addition, a Rayner inquiry conducted by an official, Christopher Joubert, devised an organizational structure which divided the DoE into 120 responsibility units or cost centres, each of which would have an annual budget that would cover running costs including those for staff. A computerized management information system would tell managers at all levels how expenditure was going against plan and a central budget unit would oversee the system and conduct systematic reviews (on a three-yearly cycle covering the whole department) of cost centre budgets. The other departments seemed less impressed with developments in the DoE than bodies like the Treasury and Civil Service Committee. The MOD, for example, was clear that it preferred its own cost control system which was literally called ABC (Acquisition, Buffer, Consumption). The permanent under secretary, Sir Frank Cooper, told the committee that in such matters the MOD tended to look at its counterparts in other western countries and not at Whitehall developments. Heseltine introduced MINIS into the MOD when he became Secretary of State for Defence and other departments were soon required to follow suit.[2]

The universalization of the MINIS and Joubert systems throughout the main central government departments formed the Thatcher government's 'grand strategy' for securing an 'efficient' civil service – Financial Management Initiative (FMI) which was launched in May 1982. The FMI's aim was described as being 'to promote in each department an organization and a system in which managers at all levels have:

(a) a clear view of their objectives; and means to assess, and wherever possible measure, outputs or performance in relation to those objectives;
(b) well-defined responsibility for making the best use of their resources, including a critical scrutiny of output and value for money; and
(c) the information (particularly about costs), the training and the access to expert advice which they need to exercise their responsibilities effectively'.

The Minister for the Civil Service, Barney Hayhoe, later emphasized that the FMI meant 'a push to greater decentralization and delegation down the line, which will represent a highly significant change in the culture of the Civil Service . . . Recruitment, training, promotion prospects and practice will all be affected.' The MPO's supporting Review of Personnel Work in the Civil Service – the Cassels Report – was published in July 1983, followed two months later by the publication of the departments' plans for implementing the FMI strategy.[3]

The recent history of British central government is littered with failed institutional developments and failed attempts to 'rationalize' its procedures – PESC and PAR and PPB. Why should the FMI succeed? In its favour, when launched, was political commitment, especially at prime ministerial level. 'We tried before, but without the clout', as one assistant secretary wrote in support of Raynerism. Essentially, the CSD was supposed to achieve the results now expected from the FMI, but was not able to do so. R. W. L. Wilding, personally involved, suggested that

> while finance was the responsibility of the Treasury and management was the responsibility of the CSD, financial management was apt to fall down the crack between the two. The CSD did its best – and not without success – to promote management accounting and internal audit, but mainly in a consulting and advisory mode. It was not until the redistribution of functions in 1981 that the leading responsibility for financial management was clearly located in the Treasury and the machinery needed for a sustained central drive could begin to be properly developed.

Even assisted by 'the clout', the prospects for the effectiveness of FMI depend upon ministerial priorities. Not all ministers are as interested in matters of departmental administration as Michael Heseltine seemed to be. They are more concerned with policy. Higher civil servants behave accordingly. Twenty years after the Plowden Report emphasized the importance of managerial responsibilities, Sir Robert Armstrong, the secretary of the Cabinet, admitted that such officials continued to find 'policy work more glamorous and more interesting than management work'. A former permanent secretary, Sir Kenneth Clucas, crisply spelt out the reality:

> To achieve a least-cost deployment of resources may be only one of a number of objectives, and in any particular case, not a top political priority. Other factors such as compatibility with the ideology of the government of the day, the attitude of important interest groups, acceptability to government backbenchers, effect on individual geographical areas, are all perfectly proper considerations for Ministers to take into account when deciding for or against any particular step. There will thus frequently be a clash between considerations of efficiency and other political priorities. Indeed it can be said that the more possible it is in any area of work to set an attainable objective, and realistically allocate a budget to it, the further away this is likely to be from current political interest and

sensitivity. There may equally be a clash between accountable management and political control. If a civil servant is to be made individually answerable for a particular area of work then it follows that he must be given the power of decision. If the exercise of that power is subject to ministerial or parliamentary direction then the individual ceases to be responsible. There are large areas over which Parliament would be unwilling to surrender control in this way, and this effectively limits the extent to which management principles can be applied.

The cost centre approach, if fully applied, would give line managers powers that would threaten what the service's critics believe to be its comfortable world of established pay scales with automatic increments, routine career expectations, and security of tenure. There is little obvious sign of this order of change, though, in the Cassels Report or the accompanying MPO material about management development in the service in the 1980s. The latter emphasized that 'the Civil Service is a career Service, i.e. its staffing policy is primarily based on recruiting people as they leave the education system and retaining them in the Service until they retire'. Not much sign here of heads rolling if the sums do not add up – and not much indication elsewhere in the material of the considerable investment in post-entry training which the detailed application of the FMI by line managers would require. The civil service has little choice about wearing the currently fashionable clothes, but much the same bodies remain underneath – and, it must be remembered, widely dispersed and still numerous ones too. More immediately threatening to the middle-rank civil servant than the FMI is the government's intention to extend unified grading down to senior principal (and, eventually, to principal level). As the SCPS recognized, this was a 'revolutionary proposal' from the standpoint of those now occupying what used to be the former executive ladder because it made that ladder more easily accessible to members of specialist groups – and, the union could have added, normally without compensating opportunities on the specialist side for generalists.[4]

Fulton had wished to maintain what it had called an 'integrated' home civil service and its unified grading proposals were part of that ambition, and the Thatcher government's action on unified grading seemed to indicate that it had no present intention of splitting up the service and thus placing it on a 'departmentalized' basis resembling the pre-Fisher structure. So did the Conservative government's behaviour in switching Treasury men and others around in the Fisher style in changes announced at permanent secretary level in late 1982. Thus far, the MOD, which has made attempts to foster greater professionalism within the administration group in the department, is the only source of serious suggestions the civil service should be split up. The effects of industrial action on defence readiness led the MOD to suggest to the Megaw Committee that a no-strike clause should be made a condition of service in the defence area; and Sir Frank Cooper as permanent under secretary, was not alone in privately favouring the establishment of a separate defence support service. The ambition expressed by one TGWU official over strike action in 1979 that 'with a little luck we will ground the Air Force' was not exceptional: but its source is a reminder that the civil service unions do not solely patrol the government departments, that they are part of a wider union movement, and that a no-strike agreement might well be only conceded in exchange for assurances about pay that would undermine one of the major purposes that the government had in confronting the civil service strike in 1981. Moreover, even if confined to the MOD, thus leaving PSA employees out, a defence support service would still be very substantial in size (222,00 in 1982, nearly half industrials) involving a multiplicity of occupational groups.[5]

What really dogs the advocacy of breaking up the home civil service is what many see as the awful example presented by the separate diplomatic service. It is not too difficult in fact to reply to the standard critique of that service. However justified in the past (even at the time of the Plowden review of overseas representation in the early 1960s) criticism of the diplomatic service preference for political rather than commercial work now seems misplaced. Even the generally critical CPRS remarked in 1977 on 'the Diplomatic Service's success in changing attitudes to export work since 1963'. As for the criticism that the service pursues a 'cult of the generalist', Plowden praised the diplomatic service for having moved away from the extreme generalism of the 1943 reforms, and proposed that officers should normally spend at least half their careers in their region or subject of specialization. The CPRS found that 'the Plowden target has more or less been met in regional specialization'. That target had been 'handsomely met in functional specialization' too, although more could be done. The CPRS was still heavily critical of the diplomatic service on most of the other familiar grounds, including the claim that British diplomats overseas had too narrow a range of contacts. That wider contacts with local populations were in some way readily available was not demonstrated, nor was evidence produced which established an association of the kind which the CPRS made between limited overseas contacts and the social ethos of the diplomatic service.[6] Whatever the evidence, though, the diplomatic service, however unfairly, still has an 'unpatriotic' taint – a hangover from the Burgess and Maclean affair – that damns it as an example that could be easily used in support of a case for breaking up the rest of the civil service.

Yet, there are some tendencies in, and features of, the home civil service which point in the direction of break-up. The abolition of the CSD took away that service's separate central personnel department. The MPO is little more than a rump organization. The Cassels Report in 1983 was clear that the MPO's role was a heavily circumscribed one – 'responsibility for developing personnel policies tailored to its needs should rest clearly with each department'.[7] Departments are now responsible for 90 per cent of direct-entry recruitment, without any reference to the traditional central authority, the Civil Service Commission. With the central Civil Service College having been the subject of recent cuts, the domination of the provision of post-entry training by departments has been emphasized. Aside from the high fliers, most civil servants are assigned to a department and stay in that broad area of work, and the frequent departures of those fliers in the Fisher manner for not necessarily related job destinations is a perennial source of criticism.[8] The structure required by the FMI bears some resemblance to the use of directorates in French central government and in the European Commission, which may be the eventual part of development. For the present, the Conservative government's 'grand strategy' for changing the civil service has gone as far as breaking down departments into their constituent parts for the purposes of cost control, and the further step of breaking up the home civil service and replacing it with departmentalized services has not been taken.

References

1 R. W. L. Wilding, 'The Post-Fulton programme: strategy and tactics', *Public Administration,* vol. 48 (1970), p. 400; Sir J. Dunnett, 'The civil service: seven years after Fulton', *Public Administration,* vol. 54 (1976), pp. 372–3; *Report of the Committee on the Civil Service* (Fulton Report) Cmnd 3638, paras 150–62, 192–243.

2 A. Likierman, 'Management information for ministers: The MINIS system in the Department of the Environment', *Public Administration,* vol. 60 (1982), pp. 127–42; G. H. Chipperfield in A. Hardcastle *et al., Management Information and Control in Whitehall* (London, 1983), pp. 22–8; *Third Report from the Treasury and Civil Service Committee. Efficiency and Effectiveness in the Civil Service,* HC 236–I (1981–2), pp. xv–xvi, xxviii, xi; HC 236–II (1981–2), pp. 108–73, 424–5, and q. 897, 1071; HC 236–III (1981–2), pp. 156–7; *Financial Management in Government Departments,* Cmnd 9058 (1983), pp. 5–16.

3 *Efficiency and Effectiveness in the Civil Service,* Cmnd 8616 (1982), pp. 5, 21–7; *House of*

Commons Weekly Hansard, no. 1271 (1983), col. 922; *Financial Management in Government Departments*, pp. 17–121.

4   P. Nash, 'We tried before, but without the clout', *Management Services in Government*, vol. 36 (1981), pp. 137–44; R. W. L. Wilding in Handcastle *et al.*, *Management Information and Control*, p. 41; HC 236–II (1981–2), q. 1226; Sir K. Clucas in J. A. G. Griffith *et al.*, *Parliament and the Executive* (London, 1982), p. 35; MPO, *Civil Service Management Development in the 1980s* (1983), paras 18–21; *Opinion*, April 1983, p. 3; *CCSU Bulletin*, April 1983, pp. 51–2.

5   *Professionalism in the Administration Group in the Ministry of Defence. Report by a Study Team* (Crew Report) (1980); Evidence by the MOD to the Megaw Committee (1981), paras 18–19; *Guardian*, 23 December 1981; *The Economist*, 8 October 1979, p. 33 (the union official being M. Martin); *Civil Service Statistics 1982*, p. 9.

6   CPRS, *Review of Overseas Representation* (1977), paras 21.11–21.13, 21.22–21.24.

7   MPO, *Review of Personnel Work in the Civil Service*, para. 10.7.

8   The MPO document, *Civil Service Management Development in the 1980s* (1983) recommends a 'general minimum period of 3–4 years in post' (para. 8).

Further Reading

In reading about the civil service the best work to start with is *Report on the Organization of the Permanent Civil Service* (1853), the Trevelyan–Northcote Report, which is to be found in *British Parliamentary Papers*, 1854, vol. 27. This report was reprinted, unfortunately without Benjamin Jowett's accompanying plan, in *Public Administration*, vol. 32 (1954), and in Appendix B to the Fulton Report. The Trevelyan–Northcote Report, despite being brief and invitingly written, seems to have been more quoted than read. This is also true of Macaulay's *Report on the Indian Civil Service*, to be found in *British Parliamentary Papers*, 1855, vol. 11 and also in Appendix B to the Fulton Report. The findings of the main reports on the civil service since the 1850s were well summarized by J. B. Bourn in *The Civil Service*, vol. 3, pt 2. *Surveys and Investigations. Evidence submitted to the Committee under the Chairmanship of Lord Fulton 1966–68*, pp. 423–65. The divided MacDonnell Royal Commission of 1912–15 did some good work, some of it taken up in the Civil Service National Whitley Council's *Report of the Joint Committee on the Organization of the Civil Service* (1920), that body's Interim (and major) Report, and a document that should be read.

The best of the history books dealing with the broad context within which the civil service developed is that by H. Parris, *Constitutional Bureaucracy. The Development of British Central Administration since the Eighteenth Century* (London, 1969). More general still is my *The Growth of Government. The Development of Ideas about the Role of the State and the Machinery and Functions of Government in Britain since 1780* (London, 1979). Of the books specifically about the civil service, two 'insider' accounts are excellent. The first is the classic study of the interwar civil service by H. E. Dale, *The Higher Civil Service of Great Britain* (London, 1941). The second is the beautifully written book by C. H. Sisson, *The Spirit of British Administration*, 2nd edn (London, 1966). The reader should also not miss Sir E. E. Bridges, *Portrait of a Profession* (London, 1950). The biggest gap in the literature is the lack of a study of Sir Warren Fisher, one that has only been partially filled by the admirable book by G. C. Peden, *British Rearmament and the Treasury 1932–39* (Edinburgh, 1979). There is valuable material, too, in the books by H. Roseveare, *The Treasury. The Evolution of a British Institution* (London, 1969), and by R. A. Chapman and J. R. Greenaway, *The Dynamics of Administrative Reform* (London, 1980). My own book, *Statesmen in Disguise. The Changing Role of the Administrative Class of the British Home Civil Service 1853–1966* (London, 1969) was described by Geoffrey Elton as 'a solidly based historical study . . . burdened with somewhat naive proposals for reform'. That book contains a long bibliography of pre-Fulton sources on the civil service.

The *Report of the Committee on the Civil Service* (Fulton Report), Cmnd 3638

(1968) has already established itself as a landmark in the development of the home civil service. Adherence to its recommendations, no matter how unwise, like those which led to the establishment of the CSD, has become the test of civil service reformism. Those of us, 'naive' reformers perhaps, who did not find the Fulton Report particularly radical where it mattered, as on post-entry training, face the risk of being counted on 'the other side'. Leading that side with apparently devilish cunning (when it mattered, frustrating reform) was Sir William Armstrong, according to P. Kellner and Lord Crowther-Hunt, *The Civil Servants. An Inquiry into Britain's Ruling Class* (London, 1980), a stimulating Fultonite tract. There is much information in another able Fultonite study by J. Garrett, *Managing the Civil Service* (London, 1980). Of the various pieces of government paper since Fulton, the English Report – the *Eleventh Report from the Expenditure Committee. The Civil Service,* HC 535–I (1976–7) – seems best remembered for the attack on the civil service made by a Minority of Labour MPs, including the above J. Garrett, led by B. Sedgemore, who subsequently wrote a book, *The Secret Constitution* (London, 1980) saying much the same thing. The evidence to the English Committee (HC 535–II, III, 1976–7) is still worth reading. Of the more recent material, the *Third Report from the Treasury and Civil Service Committee. Efficiency and Effectiveness in the Civil Service* HC 236–I (1981–2) and the accompanying evidence (HC 236–II, III, 1981–2) are valuable. Two subsequent White Papers may prove important: *Efficiency and Effectiveness in the Civil Service,* Cmnd 8616 (1982); and *Financial Management in Government Departments,* Cmnd 9058 (1983). The Management and Personnel Office (MPO) document, *Review of Personnel Work in the Civil Service* (Cassels Report) (1983) indicates the possible shape of things to come.

R. H. S. Crossman, *The Diaries of a Cabinet Minister,* 3 vols, London (1975–7) dominates any consideration of the minister–civil servant relationship. Since his death Crossman seems to have acquired a reputation for reliability that he rarely achieved in life. W. Rodgers, E. Dell, M. Rees, T. Benn and S. Williams, *Policy and Practice. The Experience of Government* (London, 1980), and J. Barnett, *Inside the Treasury* (London, 1982) contain politicians' recollections in the wake of another 'failed' Labour government. The establishment of a 'constitutional' civil service would help to avoid another 'failure' according to T. Benn, *Arguments for Democracy* (London, 1981); and that politician's views along with others are also to be found in an excellent little book by H. Young and A. Sloman, *No, Minister. An Inquiry into the Civil Service* (London, 1982). A Conservative salvo against the civil service was launched by Sir J. Hoskyns, 'Whitehall and Westminster: an outsider's view', *Parliamentary Affairs,* vol. 36 (1983), pp. 137–47. The civil servants seem capable of looking after themselves, to judge from Sir L. Pliatsky, *Getting and Spending* (Oxford, 1982). Few should want to miss reading Sir R. Clarke, *Public Expenditure, Management and Control. The Development of the Public Expenditure Survey Committee* (London, 1978). After all, the application of Clarke's ideas on the control of public spending nearly ruined the nation's finances.

The changing structure of the home civil service is difficult to plot. *Civil Service Statistics* is published annually, but only just in the same year as the figures presented. The leading administrators attract attention, but most of the rest of the service is relatively uncharted. P. Gummett, *Scientists in Whitehall* (Manchester, 1980) did his best to correct this, although, of course, most scientists in the civil service are not in Whitehall but in research establishments all over the country. The *Review of the Scientific Civil Service* (Holdgate Report), Cmnd 8032 (1980) is an informative document. As for recruitment controversies, if these were subject to rational discussion – which they are not – then they would have been settled by the *Report of the Committee on the Selection Procedure for the Recruitment of Administration Trainees* (Allen Report) which the Civil Service Commission published in 1979. The *Annual Reports* of the Civil Service Commission and of the Civil Service College are useful.

The main sources about the diplomatic service remain the three most recent substantial official studies of overseas representation. The first, the *Report of the Committee on Representational Services Overseas* (Plowden Report), Cmnd 2276 (1964) which essentially gave the service what it wanted. The second, the *Report of the Review Committee on Overseas Representation* (Duncan Report), Cmnd 4107 (1969) was afflicted by an excessive attachment to involvement with continental Europe, something only to be moderated by experience. The third, the *Review of Overseas Representation* completed by the Central Policy Review Staff in 1977, while savaged by critics, contained useful information, since supplemented by the *Second Report from the Foreign Affairs Committee. Foreign and Commonwealth Office Organization*, HC 511 (1979–80).

Essential reading on civil service pay and conditions must include the *Report of the Royal Commission on the Civil Service* (Priestley Report), Cmnd 9613 (1955), and the *Report of the Inquiry into Civil Service Pay* (Megaw Report), Cmnd 8590 (1982) and the accompanying Research Studies, Cmnd 8590–I (1982). A different view from the present writer's is available in the succinct study by P. B. Beaumont, *Government as Employer – Setting an Example?* (London, 1981).

The history of the civil service unions and of Whitleyism are well covered in B. V. Humphreys, *Clerical Unions in the Civil Service* (Oxford, 1958) and H. Parris, *Staff Relations in the Civil Service* (London, 1973) respectively. More up-to-date studies would be welcome. Two good books about individual unions are those by E. Wigham, *From Humble Petition to Militant Action: A History of the Civil and Public Services Association 1903–1978* (London, 1980) and J. E. Mortimer and V. Ellis, *A Professional Union: The Evolution of the Institution of Professional Civil Servants* (London, 1980). The unions' journals are mines of information and so is the excellent *Bulletin of the Council of Civil Service Unions* (formerly the *Whitley Bulletin*), available on subscription.

This *Bulletin* is of more use in keeping track of developments in the civil service than annual publications such as the *Civil Service Year Book* and the *Diplomatic Service List*. The newspaper and periodical coverage is now quite extensive. The quarterly *Management in Government* is the most useful of the general official publications, matched on the academic side by *Public Administration*. The *Guardian* and *The Times* follow the civil service's doings from a broadly sympathetic standpoint, and *The Economist* and the *Daily Telegraph* do so from a more antagonistic position.

Index